Discover!
Social Studies

4

edovate
LEARNING CORP

Discover! Social Studies Instructor Guide

Published in Catasauqua, Pennsylvania by Discover Press, a division of Edovate Learning Corp.

334 2nd Street

Catasauqua, PA 18032

edovate.com

ISBN: 978-1-956330-11-3

Printed in United States of America

1st Edition

Chapter 8

Chapter 9

Chapter 10

Chapter 11

Lesson Objectives

By the end of this lesson, your student will be able to:

- explain why Columbus wanted to find a new route to the Indies
- recognize that Columbus was in search of a new trade route when he landed in North America
- explain that Indigenous people lived in communities in North America before Columbus arrived

Supporting Your Student

To best support your student throughout this lesson:

- Have a world map handy. It will be helpful for your student to locate places on the map as they go through the lesson.
- Think of a few real-world deals that you could discuss in a conversation about bartering. (Examples might include doing the dishes for extra game time, trading specific Halloween candies with siblings, or a later bedtime for doing chores.)

Explore

Have several household spices ready for your student to smell and/or taste. Be prepared to discuss several ways spices are used in recipes. For example, cayenne is added to make dishes spicy, and cinnamon is used to make dishes sweet.

Write *(Why did Christopher Columbus travel to the New World? What were his goals? What did he find?)*

Help your student break up the prompt to answer each question clearly and completely. Prompt your student to refer back to the reading section to find text evidence to support their thinking. It might be helpful to begin this activity with a conversation. Allow for a range of details and opinions before discussing how your student might craft a concise written answer that directly relates to the prompt.

Practice

It might be helpful to draw a bird's eye view of your home before having your student complete this section. Before this lesson, have ideas in mind of trades you could make with your student in case they struggle to come up with ideas. For example,

you could suggest they trade their worktext at the end of the day for their baseball glove or video game controller.

Learning Styles

Auditory learners may enjoy discussing real-world examples of bartering and making fair trades with other family members.

Visual learners may enjoy exploring specific locations named in the lesson in online photos and maps. Examples include Spain, eastern Asia, and the Caribbean.

Kinesthetic learners may enjoy exploring a place around your home for the first time. For example, your student may choose to look closely at a corner of the backyard, journaling about the consistency of the dirt and the indigenous plants/animals they find. Ask them to record details of new sights, sounds, and things they find.

Extension Activities

Create a Brochure

Ask your student to revisit Christopher Columbus's findings of the plants, animals, and people in the New World. Have them pretend to be Columbus and create a brochure sharing with other European explorers what he found. They may even choose to create an advertisement on the back, persuading other explorers to travel to the New World.

Explore Your Heritage

It is likely that your student's ancestors are not indigenous to the United States. Have the student explore their heritage by creating a family tree and labeling the countries from which each member came, as far back as you can.

Travel Research

Have your student think about how and why people travel today compared to how and why Columbus traveled. List several places around the country or the world, and have your student identify how they could travel to that place today. Finally, research routes, distances, and approximate travel times to get to the places you identified.

Indigenous Plants and Animals Map

On a blank world map, have your student choose five to seven places around the world and research the indigenous plants and animals found there. Have them include pictures of their findings on the map in the appropriate locations, and then create a key to name the images.

Answer Key

Write *(Why did Christopher Columbus travel to the New World? What were his goals? What did he find?)*

Answers may vary. Possible answers: Columbus was looking for a trade route from Europe to Asia. He thought if he sailed west, he would reach the Indies in eastern Asia so that Europeans could easily trade goods, like spices. Your student might also mention that Columbus enjoyed exploring and that he dreamed of being rich and famous. Although Columbus thought he reached the Indies, he actually landed on a group of islands in the Caribbean where several Indigenous people lived. There, he also found indigenous plants and animals that he had never seen before.

Practice

Your student should draw a bird's eye view of the area that they would need to travel. Your student should draw a clear route you would take to meet each other. Possible obstacles may include walls, doorways, furniture, or landscaping.

Show What You Know

1. B
2. C
3. B
4. A
5. Answers may vary. Possible answer: Christopher Columbus did not discover America because people were already living there before he arrived. Christopher Columbus discovered America for Europe because it was a new and unfamiliar land for Europeans even though Indigenous people already lived there.

Lesson Objectives

By the end of this lesson, your student will be able to:

- describe why many European countries wanted to start colonies in North America
- find the following locations important to colonial times on a map: England, the New World (North America), the Atlantic Ocean, and Jamestown
- describe events that led to the creation of the Jamestown settlement

Supporting Your Student

Explore

Reflect with your student how early explorers and settlers like the Pilgrims traveled to the New World on large ships. One way people travel on large ships today is by cruise, but most people do not travel to the other side of the world this way. This type of reflection can get your student thinking about the ways people travel now and the reasons why they travel may be similar to or different from the early settlers.

Write (Describe the advantages and disadvantages of settling near the James River.)

To support your student in responding to this question, remind them to return to the text sections under the heading "The Beginnings of Jamestown." Have your student highlight reasons the colonists believed the James River was a good location. If they are struggling, tell them to pay close attention to the details about hunting, fishing, and safety. After reading about the advantages of their location, help your student to understand the importance of the following sentence: "Unfortunately, the settlers soon found out the location of their new home had many disadvantages." This sentence indicates that they will be reading about disadvantages in the sentences that follow. They should note details about how the proximity of the river to the ocean made the river water salty, that the mosquitoes carried malaria, and that the settlers found it difficult to plant crops.

Practice

Remind your student that sequencing means putting details in order. Walk them through the section of text under the heading "The Beginnings of Jamestown." After reading that John Smith guided a group of people to Jamestown from England, stop to model a think-aloud. It might sound something like this: "John Smith guided people to Jamestown from England. This sounds like an important event in the establishment of the colony. I'm going to highlight it and put a number 1 in the margin to show that this is the first step in starting the colony." Have your student continue reading and thinking aloud until they get to the second event: that the group chose to build a fort on the James River. Remind your student to place a number 2 in the margin to label it the second important event. Continue this way until your student finds all six events. In the practice activity, compare highlighted details from the text to the statements written in this Practice section. The wording may not be exact, but the idea is the same. Have your student write the number they identified for each highlighted detail next to the corresponding statement in this section. Then, have your student order the statements correctly in the sequencing boxes provided. If your student wishes, they could draw a picture near each statement as a visual.

Learning Styles

Auditory learners may enjoy listening to a song or poem about a topic unique to the early colonies: Indigenous people, Jamestown, England, or nature.

Visual learners may enjoy creating a poster with images and details about Pocahontas or another prominent figure from the Jamestown settlement.

Kinesthetic learners may enjoy acting out some of the actions described in the reading, such as planting or building a fort.

Extension Activities

Compare/Contrast

In this lesson, your student learned a little bit about Pocahontas and John Smith. If they have seen a popular movie about Pocahontas, they may have some questions about conflicting information. Ask your student to do some research about Pocohontas on a computer by searching for relevant kid-friendly articles or videos to learn more about her. Then have your student compare a popular movie about Pocahontas to their own research based on historical facts.

Warning Sign

In 1607, the world did not have advanced studies in science to tell people how dangerous tobacco could be. In modern times, we have a lot of information at our disposal that helps us understand the implications of smoking and vaping. Have your student research the effects smoking could have on people's health and create a poster warning others about the dangers of smoking and tobacco. Then have your student create a flyer or write a letter that could have been given to the colonies to warn them of these dangers.

Come One, Come All

Have your student look back at previous lessons about colonies in the New World: Plymouth, Massachusetts Bay, and Jamestown. Ask them to create an advertisement that encourages other Europeans to move to one of these colonies in the New World. They might include information about the colony's location, climate, natural resources, European settlers, and Indigenous people.

Answer Key

Explore

Answers will vary depending on where your student chooses to travel to.

Write (Describe the advantages and disadvantages of settling near the James River.)

Answers will vary. Possible answers include:

Advantages: They could hunt and fish in the James River. The location was hidden from ocean attacks. It was safe from any attacks by Indigenous people.

Disadvantages: Salt in the river water made the water undrinkable. Mosquitoes carrying malaria made people sick. They did not know how to plant crops successfully.

Practice

4: John Smith bartered with local Indigenous people to trade tools for food.

2: Colonists set up a fort on the James River.

5: The Virginia Company sent indentured servants to Jamestown.

1: John Smith led men from England to the New World to start the colony of Jamestown.

3: Many men got sick from drinking the river water, and some died of malaria.

6: Colonists learned that tobacco grew well in Virginia and was worth a lot to Europeans.

Show What You Know

2. A

3. C

4. B

5. D

6. D

7. B

8. A

9. 4: John Smith returned to England. While he was gone, the settlers suffered a cold winter.
2: Settlers built a fort on the James River.
6: Jamestown became successful, not for gold but for the tobacco that grew well in the area.
1: A man named John Smith guided a group of people to Jamestown from England.
3: Settlers became sick from drinking water from the James River and got diseases from mosquitoes.
5: Indentured servants arrived in the New World and worked on large plantations.

Lesson Objectives

By the end of this lesson, your student will be able to:

- describe ways the king of England controlled English churches and their members
- explain why the Pilgrims traveled to and settled in North America
- describe the challenges the Pilgrims had in Plymouth, including why the first winter was very hard for the Pilgrims
- identify how Indigenous people helped the Pilgrims survive in America

Supporting Your Student

Explore *(Sidebar)*

Encourage your student to brainstorm several reasons they think Europeans may have been motivated to travel to the New World. Remind them that Christopher Columbus shared stories of the land, fruits, vegetables, animals, and the natives. See if your student can name potential needs, wants, and ways the Europeans may have been persuaded by others before them. Here are some examples to discuss:

- Needs: Europeans may have needed more land, new opportunities, or freedoms.
- Wants: They might have wanted to trade goods other than spices, to conquer land, and to seek the same fame and fortune that Columbus had by exploring and mapping the new land.
- Persuasion: Many Europeans journeyed to the New World and shared their experiences with friends and relatives back home. As curiosity grew, more and more Europeans planned explorations of their own. Some Europeans believed there was gold in the New World. They persuaded others to travel and search for it in hopes they would become rich.

Write *(What motivated the Pilgrims to move to the New World?)*

It might be helpful to begin this activity with a conversation. Begin by discussing the definition of "motivation" and ask your student to come up with some realistic examples to make connections. Model some thinking aloud for your student if necessary. When they're ready to write, remind your student to refer back to the reading sections to find text evidence to support their thinking. Discuss how your student might use details from the reading, like "The Pilgrims did not want to change their beliefs or live with the threat of prison or death" to craft a concise written answer that directly relates to the prompt.

Practice

In this activity, your student is asked to design a comic strip to illustrate the challenges Pilgrims faced during their first winter in Plymouth and how they overcame the challenges. If your student isn't familiar with comics, you may choose to have a few handy or use a search engine to find some comics online that provide some illustrative examples.

It might help to plan out each frame before they start by asking which three details they think are important. They may choose ideas such as:

- It was too cold to find materials and build homes, so many Pilgrims slept on the Mayflower.
- The ground was frozen, so the Pilgrims couldn't plant crops.
- The Pilgrims were unfamiliar with the land and didn't know how to hunt or fish.
- Due to the harsh winter, over half of the group died.
- In the spring, the Pilgrims were able to start building their homes.
- The local Indigenous people taught the Pilgrims how to hunt, fish, and plant crops.
- The Pilgrims and the Indigenous people traded things they had for things they wanted.

LESSON 3
Pilgrims

Learning Styles

Auditory learners may enjoy listening to a story about the first Thanksgiving. There are many books available on the subject, as well as audio recordings and videos.

Visual learners may enjoy watching a video or documentary about topics such as shipbuilding or Indigenous people of North America. They might also want to make their own video about the arrival of the Pilgrims at Plymouth.

Kinesthetic learners may enjoy making a meal with foods grown by the Pilgrims, such as squash, beans, and corn.

Extension Activities

Harvesting Plants
Have your student plant seeds, make daily observations, and care for their own "crops." Make connections to how the Pilgrims may have harvested their own food.

Write a Legend
After reading the legend of the "three sisters," have your student write their own legend about a topic in which they're interested (perhaps a topic that is connected to your student's family, friends, or the area in which they live).

Research Places to Live
Ask your student to think about what would motivate people to live in various parts of the country or the world. Look up several locations online to research what they have to offer and discuss why those things might motivate people to move there.

Answer Key

Write *(What motivated the Pilgrims to move to the New World?)*
Answers will vary. Possible answers: The Pilgrims were motivated to move to the New World for religious freedom. They wanted to separate from the Church of England and practice religion in their own way. The first winter was very difficult for the Pilgrims, and many people died. Through their first year, they may have been motivated to learn to plant crops and build shelters to avoid more deaths or a failed colony.

Practice
Answers may vary. Possible drawings: Pilgrims arriving on the Mayflower, a cold and harsh winter, many deaths among the Pilgrims, homes built out of materials from the land, the Wampanoag people helping the Pilgrims grow food

Show What You Know
1. A, C, D

2.

CAUSE		EFFECT
The Pilgrims wanted freedom to practice their religion the way they wanted.	→	A group of Pilgrims decided to move so they could practice their religion without fear of prison or death.
The Pilgrims arrived in the New World during a very cold winter.	→	The Pilgrims could not plant crops and had few options for shelter.
The Wampanoag people were familiar with the land and how to grow crops.	→	The people helped the Pilgrims become successful at harvesting crops.

3. A, C

4. Answers will vary. Possible answers: The first winter was difficult for the Pilgrims because it was so cold. The Pilgrims had a hard time building shelters and planting crops in the frozen ground. They were unfamiliar with the land and its resources. They didn't know how to hunt animals or use their fur for warmth.

Lesson Objectives

By the end of this lesson, your student will be able to:

- identify the important agreement the government of Plymouth had in the colony
- describe why the Mayflower Compact was important to the Plymouth colony and the early formation of the country

Supporting Your Student

Explore

Your student will begin this lesson by exploring the idea of conflict resolution to get them thinking about the creation of rules and laws. Remind your student that Pilgrims on the *Mayflower* lived and slept in close quarters when they sailed over the Atlantic. Brainstorm with your student about what kinds of disagreements may have arisen. To make this relevant, ask your student to brainstorm times when they may have disagreed with a sibling or friend about something. How did they solve the conflict if no one was there to problem-solve with them? Ask if they came up with an agreement or a rule that they would follow to avoid future conflicts.

Read (The Need for a Plan)

All of the vocabulary words are defined in the reading. If your student is struggling to remember the definitions, write them on note cards and have them accessible throughout the lesson. Remind your student that *compact* has several synonyms, including *promise*, *agreement*, and *contract*.

Write (Describe the document that the Pilgrims used as their first form of government. Why was this document so important to the Plymouth colony?)

Guide your student in recognizing the two parts of this question. First, they need to recall that the document written by the Pilgrims was called the Mayflower Compact. Have them return to the text to find and highlight important information to describe it. The next part of the question requires some deeper thinking. If your student is struggling to use details about the Mayflower Compact to understand why it was so important, ask guiding questions such as, "How did the Mayflower Compact help the Pilgrims?" or "What rules in the Mayflower Compact would have helped ensure Plymouth was successful?" It might be helpful to model thinking aloud for your student before encouraging them to share their ideas.

Practice

In this activity, your student is asked to write and sign a compact with a parent or sibling. Encourage them to be creative and to come up with several ideas before choosing one. Ideas may include going to bed later if they agree to do the dishes for a week or letting a sibling choose a movie if they agree to do something in return.

Learning Styles

Auditory learners may enjoy listening to an audio recording of the Mayflower Compact being read online.

Visual learners may enjoy watching a documentary about the history of democratic ideas in the United States.

Kinesthetic learners may enjoy reenacting what they imagine the conversation was like between the Pilgrims as they signed the Mayflower Compact.

Extension Activities

Analyze the Primary Document

Use a computer to find a video or image of the Mayflower Compact. See if your student can pull out the big ideas from the actual wording of the document and put them in their own words. For example, "combine ourselves together into a civil Body Politick" means that the men agreed to form a government ruled by themselves.

Create a Timeline

As your student learns about more events in American history, it might be helpful to create a large timeline to refer to and add to as the lessons progress.

Write a Family Compact

Just as the men on the *Mayflower* wrote an agreement for a group to follow, your student might find it fun

LESSON 4
Plymouth Colony

to write a compact for the whole family. Include agreements that fit your household and routines, such as how long the TV is on each day.

Answer Key

Explore
Answers will vary. Possible answers:

- Disagreement: We got into a fight over a toy and did not talk. Solution: We made a deal to end the conflict.
- Disagreement: We got angry at each other and started to say mean things. Solution: We apologized for our behavior and shook hands.
- Disagreement: One of us said something funny and the other person got offended. Solution: We explained to each other what we were thinking.

Write (What types of disagreements do you think the colonists had in Plymouth?)
Answers will vary. Possible answers:

- Some may have complained they did not have enough room on the *Mayflower*.
- Some may have taken more than their fair share of food.
- Maybe there was not someone in charge to help resolve the conflicts, or maybe too many people wanted to be the leader.
- Maybe they disagreed about how to build their homes.

Write (Describe the document that the Pilgrims used as their first form of government. Why was this document so important to the Plymouth colony?)
Answers will vary. Possible answers:

- The Mayflower Compact was an agreement signed on the *Mayflower* by the Pilgrims before they arrived in Plymouth.
- The Pilgrims promised to act in ways that was good for everyone and to make fair laws while they lived in Plymouth.
- The men would choose a leader who they promised to obey.

- The document was important because everyone who signed it agreed to its rules.
- By acting in ways that were good for the colony and by obeying their leader, Plymouth was eventually successful.
- The Mayflower Compact was the first example of democracy in our country. It was an early model of the type of government we still have today.
- The Mayflower Compact gave each man in the colony a say in how the colony should be run by establishing a government ruled by the people.

Practice
Answers will vary. In comparing the agreement to the Mayflower Compact, some responses may include:

- Our agreement is signed by two people, while the Mayflower Compact was signed by several adults.
- Our agreement only works in our home for our family. The Mayflower Compact defined rules for an entire community.
- The Mayflower Compact was a long-term promise that helped make the colony successful. Our agreement is just for fun.
- Our agreement is similar to the Mayflower Compact because each agreement is a form of democracy.

Show What You Know
1. compact
2. colony
3. democracy
4. Mayflower
5. False
6. True
7. True

Lesson Objectives

By the end of this lesson, your student will be able to:

- describe how life was different for people who moved to North America
- state the meaning of the word *barter*
- explain how the Indigenous people used their natural surroundings to survive and barter
- compare and contrast how the Indigenous people and settlers viewed owning land
- compare and contrast the Pilgrims with the Indigenous people they encountered
- describe how the lives of the Indigenous people changed because of colonial settlements

Supporting Your Student

Explore

In this activity, your student is asked to compare themselves with another person. Help them brainstorm a list of people they know well (maybe a sibling, a parent, a friend, or a grandparent). Explain how a Venn diagram works if they need more explanation than the directions give. A Venn diagram is a visual way of comparing two things, and it helps people organize their thinking. A Venn diagram shows differences on the right and left and similarities in the middle where the circles overlap. *Comparing* means finding differences and similarities. Start by having a conversation about how your student is different from the person they chose. If they only name physical characteristics, push them to think about qualities in each that can't be seen. You might ask, "Are your favorite foods the same or different?" or "Do you have any personality traits in common? Which personality traits are different?"

This activity leads to an in-depth comparison of the Indigenous people and the Pilgrims. Your student might find it helpful to review what they learned about the Pilgrims from earlier lessons.

Write *(In what ways were the Pilgrims and the Indigenous people different?)*

Model for your student how to highlight specific details in the text that describe differences between the Pilgrims and the Indigenous people. If your student is struggling to use details to understand their differences, ask guiding questions such as "What kinds of tools did the Pilgrims/Indigenous people use?" or "What kind of transportation did the Pilgrims/Indigenous people use?" It might be helpful to model some thinking aloud for your student. Then, encourage them to share their ideas. Possible responses are in the Answer Key section.

Practice

Help your student label North America and Europe on the map before analyzing the Columbian Exchange. Remind them that foods like grapes, bananas, and olives didn't grow naturally in North America until they were introduced during this time period. Likewise, turkeys weren't native to Europe. Encourage your student to think how each continent was impacted positively and negatively by the Columbian Exchange. Talking it out will help them write their ideas down later.

Learning Styles

Auditory learners may enjoy writing and then singing a song about the Columbian Exchange.

Visual learners may enjoy watching an online video or documentary about the Columbian Exchange. (Tip: Search "Columbian Exchange for kids.")

Kinesthetic learners may enjoy acting out a possible scenario in which Pilgrims barter with the Indigenous people. Since the Indigenous people were familiar with the land and were expert hunters, they might offer to trade a warm animal skin coat for some metal cooking pots or sharp tools.

Extension Activities

Make a Recipe

Through the analysis of the Columbian Exchange map and additional research, have your student find and make a recipe from foods that only came from Europe or from foods that only came from North America.

Make a Health Connection

Research the background of some of the diseases listed on the Columbian Exchange map. Compare one of them to a current illness children or adults may experience. Research, discuss, and compare strategies used to help people avoid getting the disease or remedies to cure it.

Answer Key

Explore

Answers will vary. Possible answers:

- physical trait similarities and differences, including hair color, eye color, height, gender, clothing preferences, glasses, braces, or age
- personality trait similarities and differences, including fears, strengths, food preferences, entertainment preferences, or desires for the future

In thinking about what your student has learned about the Pilgrims and the Indigenous people in previous lessons, they might list various similarities including:

- They both lived in the New World around Plymouth, Massachusetts.
- They both grew crops to eat.
- They both built their own homes.

Various differences may include:

- The Indigenous people had lived in North America for a long time.
- The Pilgrims had lived in England before they moved to the New World.
- The Pilgrims were Christians who moved for religious freedom.
- The Indigenous people knew the land they lived on well.

Write (In what ways were the Pilgrims and Indigenous people different?)

Answers may vary. Possible answers:

- The Indigenous people believed in sharing the land

and its resources, while the Pilgrims believed it should be owned by individuals.

- Pilgrims built fences around their homes to create boundaries for their property.
- The Pilgrims used metal tools, while the Indigenous people only used what they could make from the land.
- The Indigenous people were very familiar with the land and were expert hunters and fishermen. The Pilgrims were new to the area and didn't know how to use the land to survive.
- The Pilgrims sailed on a ship called the Mayflower, and the Indigenous people used small row boats.
- The Pilgrims and the Indigenous people dressed very differently.

Practice

Possible answers for "From the New World to Europe":

tobacco, pumpkin, quinine, turkey, squash, pineapple, sweet potato, avocado, peppers, cacao bean, cassava, peanut, potato, tomato, corn, beans, and vanilla

Possible answers for "From Europe to the New World":

coffee bean, peach, pear, olive, banana, citrus fruit, sugar cane, onion, turnip, grape, grains, livestock, and diseases

Show What You Know

1. C
2. B
3. A
4. B
5. B, C
6. Answers will vary. Possible answers: Life was different for people who moved to North America for many reasons. The Pilgrims had to learn to live off the land by building their own homes and harvesting crops to eat. They had to learn to hunt, fish, and survive from the local Indigenous people. The Pilgrims had to learn to barter in the New World and may not have had the kinds of tools and supplies they had in Europe.

Lesson Objectives

By the end of this lesson, your student will be able to:

- identify the reasons why the Puritans left England and went to the New World
- describe daily life in the Puritan communities
- compare and contrast the Massachusetts Bay Colony and the Plymouth Colony
- describe the laws the Puritans made

Supporting Your Student

Explore

This activity asks your student to explore unusual laws or rules that do not make sense to them. It might be helpful to pull a list of unusual laws that are kid-friendly from the internet before beginning the lesson or to brainstorm a list of rules that your student can connect to. If your student struggles to identify rules they disagree with in their own lives, ask them to think about rules that apply to kids in general by asking, "What rules do kids have to follow in different places, like at the grocery store or at church?" and "Do you agree with all of the rules kids have to follow in these places?"

Write *(Describe daily life in the Puritan communities.)*

To support your student in responding to this question, remind them to return to the text section under the heading "Daily Life for the Puritans." Reread the section out loud to show your student how to find relevant information. When you get to the sentence "The Puritans were Christians who believed in reading and following the Bible in their everyday lives," stop and think aloud. You might say something like, "Interesting. Puritans believed in living their everyday lives according to the Bible. To me, this means their faith was important to them. It also might mean they were very well-behaved. Let's highlight this so we can come back to it when we write the paragraph." Continue reading through the paragraph with your student, stopping to think about phrases that describe their daily lives.

Practice

Have two or three different colored highlighters or pencils handy for this activity. With your student, reread through the text sentence by sentence, highlighting text and recording short notes in the table. When finding evidence in the text, be sure to mark near the detail whether it refers to Pilgrims or Puritans if you are using the same color for the differences.

Learning Styles

Auditory learners may enjoy recording a podcast about what life was like in Plymouth Colony or Massachusetts Bay Colony.

Visual learners may enjoy making an infographic to compare the Pilgrims and Puritans, using words and pictures.

Kinesthetic learners may enjoy building a model of the Plymouth Colony and the Massachusetts Bay Colony with toy blocks.

Extension Activities

Research

In the 1600s, the Puritans believed that there were people who practiced witchcraft in their colony. Ask your student to find out the "who, what, where, when, and why" of the Salem Witch Trials, which took place in colonial Salem, Massachusetts from 1692 to 1693. They might watch kid-friendly videos online, read kid-friendly articles online, or find relevant books at the public library, for example. Ask your student to create some type of visual presentation that shares images and information about the Salem Witch Trials. They may choose to do this digitally or on paper.

Puritan Poetry

Have your student learn about Anne Bradstreet—the first female poet in North America. Anne Bradstreet was a Puritan, and many of her poems reflect her religious beliefs. Your student may choose to find out more about Anne Bradstreet herself or may choose to analyze one of her poems. Choose a stanza, or paragraph, of the poem and ask your student to put it into their own words. They may also choose to write a main idea about a poem or identify a theme.

Dear America

Explore the *Dear America* book series for fictional journals told by characters in Plymouth or Massachusetts Bay between 1620 and 1700.

Answer Key

Explore

Answers will vary. Possible answers:

- In the state of West Virginia, only babies can ride in strollers.
- It is against the law to sleep in a refrigerator in Pennsylvania.
- Kids cannot wear pajamas to school.
- Kids cannot use the oven when parents are not home.

Write *(Describe daily life in the Puritan communities.)*

Answers will vary. Possible answers: The Puritans lived very godly lives. They read and followed the teachings of the Bible every day. The Puritan people had a very strong work ethic. They worked hard in their homes and on their land. They behaved properly and followed strict rules. The Puritans did not get along well with the Indigenous people.

Practice

Answers will vary. Possible responses include:

PILGRIMS	BOTH	PURITANS
-Arrived in the New World in 1620	-Wanted religious freedom	-Arrived in the New World in 1630
-Wanted to separate from the Church of England	-Worked hard to make their colonies successful	-Wanted to purify the Church of England
-Plymouth Colony	-Built their own homes and planted their own food	-Massachusetts Bay Colony
-Many died during the first winter		-More prepared
-Created alliances with natives and relied on them to survive the first winter		-More educated and had more money
		-Did not get along well with the natives
		-Followed very strict laws

Show What You Know

1. C
2. F
3. A
4. B
5. D
6. E
7. B, D
8. A, C, D

Lesson Objectives

By the end of this lesson, your student will be able to:

- identify the New England colonies, the Middle colonies, and the Southern colonies and locate them on a map
- identify important colonial leaders and people
- describe the location of the Thirteen Colonies as being on the east coast
- identify examples of common colonial jobs in the New England colonies, the Middle colonies, and the Southern colonies
- compare and contrast colonial life with how people live today

Supporting Your Student

Explore

Explain to your student that *modern* means "common" in today's world. Conveniences are things that make our lives easier. Go through the examples given and challenge your student to imagine how each machine's job was done before the technology existed. For example, the microwave did not exist until long after the Pilgrims arrived in the New World. How did they cook their food? Without electricity, they would have had to use fire. Have your student draw a small picture to illustrate using fire before microwaves existed. After talking through the other examples, see if your student can come up with a couple examples of other modern conveniences. Ideas could include video games or other forms of entertainment for kids, refrigerators, or showers.

Write *(Which region of the Thirteen Colonies would you have wanted to live?)*

To support your student in responding to this question, have them summarize the different characteristics of each of the regions. Then have them think about which characteristics match with things that they like to do. For example, if your student likes to garden or grow things, they might have enjoyed living in the Southern colonies where farming was important and they grew cash crops.

Practice

To assist your student with filling in the chart, remind them to return to the text on the previous pages. Help them by starting under the heading "Common Colonial Jobs." Read sentence-by-sentence, highlighting pertinent information, such as "In the 1600s and 1700s, colonists did not have the machines and technology we have today. They had to make everything by hand." From this sentence, your student might write "We have technology" under the Life Today section and "Made everything by hand" under the Colonial Life section.

Continue working through the text to highlight details and add information to the chart. With each new detail, push your student to compare what life was like in colonial days to life now. To do this, ask them to give an example or explanation of how a similar act is done today. For colonial jobs, your student might write that a miller made grains and wheat into flour. Today, someone who makes baked goods to sell would probably buy flour from a store or order a large quantity online.

Learning Styles

Auditory learners may enjoy writing and rehearsing a poem about a region of the colonies or specific colonial jobs.

Visual learners may enjoy watching a documentary or other video with living history actors portraying life in the colonies.

Kinesthetic learners may enjoy doing a colonial job by hand, such as washing clothes or making an item of clothing.

Extension Activities

Start A Business

What did it take for colonists to start their own businesses? A lot of planning, preparation, and materials. Ask your student what kind of business they would start. A lemonade stand? Selling crafts? Sewing small items? Then have your student make a plan and try out their business!

Research a City

Have your student choose a city on the east coast they are particularly interested in. Have them do research and create a timeline with visuals to explain the history of the city.

Answer Key

Explore

Drawings will vary.

Write *(Which region of the Thirteen Colonies would you want to live?)*

Answers will vary. Possible answers: The New England colonies offered religious freedom. The Middle colonies were the most welcoming and the best region for farming and starting businesses. The Southern colonies made a lot of money on crops that grew well there. The New England colonies had many forests and were popular for shipbuilding and fishing. The Southern colonies were the farthest south and the warmest. The colony of Georgia was set up to help people, so I would live in the Southern colonies.

Practice

Answers will vary. Possible answers:

(Colonial Life) People made almost everything by hand. People worked to make things that helped people survive, such as food and clothing. Most women worked in or close to the home.

(Both) People choose specific places to live. Some people build their own homes or choose to make their own clothes. Some items we need (food, clothing, shelter, etc.) are the same — they are just made differently now.

(Life Today) Technology helps us make many products. People buy food and clothing from a store. Many women work outside of the house in jobs similar to men.

Show What You Know

1. New England colonies: Massachusetts, Connecticut, New Hampshire, and Rhode Island
   Middle colonies: Pennsylvania, New York, New Jersey, and Delaware
   Southern colonies: Maryland, Virginia, North Carolina, South Carolina, and Georgia

2. Blue: New England colonies
   Red: Middle colonies
   Yellow: Southern colonies

3. east

4. Georgia

5. Pennsylvania

6. True

7. False

8. False

9. True

10. Answers will vary. Possible answers: People still choose where they want to live. Some people still build their own homes. Some people still grow their own food, make their own clothing, etc.

11. Answers will vary. Possible answers:

    • Colonial people could find blacksmiths, tailors, or cobblers if they needed something, but everything was made by hand. We can just go to the store if we need to buy something.

    • There were no machines to make clothing or print newspapers. Today, we have technology to produce large amounts of products at a time.

    • Women did many chores around the house. They did laundry by hand, took care of the children, and made food like butter. Today, many women work in all kinds of jobs outside of the home.

    • Most colonists made what they could at home. We buy a lot at the grocery store.

Lesson Objectives

By the end of this lesson, your student will be able to:
- identify important waterways in the colonies
- describe how colonists use different waterways and their importance

Supporting Your Student

Explore

Help your student brainstorm ways people might use waterways today by thinking about activities they, family members, or friends have done on or near water. For example, you might ask them to recall a trip to an ocean, river, or lake that their family took and what they did there.

Read

As your student reads the lesson materials, help them connect what they are reading to current-day uses of waterways. For example, you might point out that people still use waterways for trading and moving from place to place. Today, however, the boats and ships people use are usually powered by an engine and are often larger.

Write *(Why were major rivers and waterways important to early settlers in the colonies?)*

To support your student in responding to this question, help them bring together several details they learned in the lesson so far. Model for your student how to return to the text and highlight information that is pertinent to the question. For example, you might highlight details that mention the colonists using fresh water found in rivers for drinking or how they relied on rivers to help them move quickly from place to place to trade.

Learning Styles

Auditory learners may enjoy telling a story about early colonists through the perspective of a freshwater fish who is watching the colonists move around on a river.

Visual learners may enjoy creating a diagram that compares how colonists used natural sources of water to how their family uses them today.

Kinesthetic learners may enjoy visiting a local lake, river, or stream to study the ground around it for moisture.

Extension Activities

Water as a Source of Energy

Today, technology allows us to do a lot more with fresh water than people could in the 1600s and 1700s. Have your student research and create a presentation about energy that comes from water or wastewater treatment.

Gardening

Have your student create an experiment to see how plants grow with different levels of water in the soil. Consider having three or four different pots with seeds and watering them in varying amounts from no water to constantly soaked. Connect this to why colonists lived near rivers where the soil was more fertile.

Hydroponics

Have your student research how hydroponics (or gardening without soil) works. Have them create a presentation that includes diagrams, drawings, or descriptions. You may even consider having your student try this type of gardening at home to record daily observations.

Answer Key

Explore

Answers will vary. Possible answers: swimming, fishing, waterskiing, boating, scuba diving, parasailing, surfing, paddleboarding

Write *(Why were major rivers and waterways important to early settlers in the colonies?)*

Answers will vary. Possible answers: Rivers and waterways were important for several reasons. Settlers used fresh water for everyday needs, such as drinking, bathing, and washing clothes. They also fished in the rivers and relied on them to lure animals to the water so the settlers could hunt them. Settlers also used rivers to get from place to place by boat. Early explorers used them to get farther inland so they could map the land. Many settlers traveled and traded with nearby communities by way of rivers. Another reason waterways were important to settlers in the colonies was that the land around the rivers was moist and created fertile ground for growing crops. This was especially true in the Middle Colonies and Southern Colonies.

Practice

Drawings will vary. Possible drawings: colonists fishing or hunting near a river, colonists traveling on a boat, colonists getting drinking water or washing clothes

Show What You Know

1. C
2. B
3. A
4. True
5. True
6. False
7. True
8. True
9. False
10. True

Lesson Objectives

By the end of this lesson, your student will be able to:

- state the meaning of the words *imports* and *exports*
- identify cash crops (tobacco, rice, and indigo) that the Southern Colonies exported and where they were grown
- describe why cash crops were important to Southern Colonies like Virginia and the Carolinas
- describe the reasons for the rise of slavery in the colonies
- describe why Charles Town was important to the Southern Colonies' economy

Supporting Your Student

Explore

Explain to your student that not everything they need or want can be made in the United States. Sometimes products they buy could be made in another part of the world. Show your student an example by finding an item in your home that has a label or tag starting with "Made in."

Look at the table in the Explore section and talk through the directions with your student. On their scavenger hunt, they will continue looking for labels that indicate where items in their home were made. If they find an item made in a country that is not listed in the table, have them write the name of the country in the left column on one of the blank lines.

To help your student draw conclusions about their scavenger hunt, ask them guiding questions such as, "Are most items in our home imported from another country?" or "From what country outside of the United States did you tally the most?" You might also have them gather a few similar items, such as items of clothing, to see if they were made in the same country. Then you might ask them why one country might focus on producing clothing or how that could benefit them and the countries that they trade with. Doing so could help your student to explore the concept of international trade more thoroughly and effectively.

Write *(Explain the Triangle Trade system. Include the words* imports *and* exports.*)*

If your student is struggling to understand the terms *imports* and *exports*, you may consider visually showing them the word parts of each. You could provide your student with the tip that *im-* sounds like "in." *Importing* means bringing goods in. *Ex-*, as in "exit" and "exterior," means "out." *Exporting* means taking goods out of a country. On the maps in this lesson, use two different colors to show the importing and exporting routes of North America. Have your student return to the text and to the Triangle Trade map to highlight specific information that helps them answer the prompt. If more guidance is necessary, ask questions such as, "What three continents were involved in the triangle?" or "What was exported from each continent?"

Practice

Your student should refer back to the Triangle Trade map in the lesson if they are struggling to remember what exports were shipped out of each continent. To stretch your student's thinking, ask them why they think that this process of trading benefited all of the countries that were involved in it.

Learning Styles

Auditory learners may enjoy listening to podcasts, books, or stories about experiences of slaves. Popular elementary titles include *The Road to Freedom* and *Henry's Freedom Box*.

Visual learners may enjoy creating a map to show how importing and exporting work. They might also enjoy drawing pictures of some of the different goods that are imported and exported from a few different countries to make the map more colorful and interesting.

Kinesthetic learners may enjoy participating in a role play about importing and exporting. They may make a craft or small project in one room and "export" it to another room. Then they could "trade" it with something in that room and bring it back to the original room to demonstrate "importing."

Extension Activities

Start a Business

To help your student understand aspects of the economy better, you may suggest they start a small business of their own, such as a lemonade stand. Encourage your student to create a plan explaining how their product will be made and sold. Have them keep track of how much they spend on materials to set up their business and how much they earn from it. Encourage your student to make connections to the larger economy by asking questions such as, "Where do toys and games come from before they are bought in stores?" or "Where does the money you pay go after your purchase?"

The Supply Chain

Many businesses must purchase materials from other businesses or countries in order to get the supplies that they need to make their products. Help your student choose a familiar product (i.e., a favorite toy, favorite food) and access that business' website. Many businesses include information on their suppliers, where they get their materials, the sustainability of the materials that they use, etc. Explore how many materials are used in making the product that they have chosen and how the importing and exporting of materials plays an important role in the creation and production of that product.

Port Research

Have your student choose a big port in the United States, such as the Port of Houston or Port Newark. Have them use a computer to look at real-world images and then find out what kinds of goods are imported and exported through the ports today. Ask your student to find out where ships go when they leave the port. Online videos may help your student better visualize how ships are loaded at a port.

Answer Key

Explore

Answers will vary. Possible answers: Many of the items were made in the US, China, or India. Some items were made in countries that are very far away. One country produced a lot of the same item, such as clothing or toys. Many products are made in other countries and have traveled a long, long way before ending up in a home.

Write (Explain the Triangle Trade system. Include the words imports and exports.)

Answers will vary. Possible answers: The Triangle Trade was a system of trading between North America, Europe, and Africa, starting in the 1600s. Each country received imports from another place and exported goods. North America exported cash crops—the crops that grew well in the Southern Colonies—including cotton, rice, indigo, and tobacco to Europe. Europe took those crops and turned them into manufactured goods, such as clothing, and exported them to Africa. Africa exported slaves to North America to work in plantations and produce more crops. This system introduced slavery to the colonies as more plantation owners learned they could produce more crops with more workers in the fields.

Practice

On the map, North America is on the upper left-hand side, Europe is on the upper right-hand side, and Africa is on the lower right-hand side. Where the lines meet in North America, that point should be labeled "Charles Town." There should be arrows indicating that products from North America were exported to Europe, that products from Europe were exported to Africa, and that products from Africa were exported to North America. The line from North America to Europe should be labeled "cash crops such as tobacco, rice, cotton, indigo." The line from Europe to Africa should be labeled "manufactured goods." The line from Africa to North America should be labeled "slaves."

Show What You Know

1. A
2. B
3. C
4. C
5. A
6. C

Lesson Objectives

In this lesson, your student will review the following big ideas from Chapter 1.

- Columbus landed in North America while searching for a new trade route. (Lesson 1)
- Jamestown was the first permanent English settlement in the New World. (Lesson 2)
- The Pilgrims and Puritans both came to settle in the New World, but they were different in many ways. (Lessons 3 and 6)
- The Mayflower Compact was a document that outlined how Plymouth Colony would be governed, and it still influences American government today. (Lesson 4)
- Indigenous people were impacted by the arrival of settlers in the New World. (Lesson 5)
- The colonies were divided into three regions that each had unique characteristics: New England Colonies, Middle Colonies, and Southern Colonies. (Lesson 7)
- There were many waterways in the colonies that were important to the colonists for survival and transportation. (Lesson 8)
- Cash crops were important to the Southern Colonies and an important part of the Triangle Trade with Europe and Africa. (Lesson 9)

Supporting Your Student

Review

As your student reads the Review sections, it may be helpful for them to stop after each subsection and summarize what they read either verbally or in writing. For example, after reading about the New World, guide your student to first discuss why Columbus ended up in the New World and how his "discovery" affected both people in Europe and the Indigenous people already living in the New World. Then have them summarize how the first three settlements began: Jamestown, Plymouth, and Massachusetts Bay.

Practice (Visualizing Vocabulary)

If your student struggles to come up with drawings to represent the words, have them brainstorm other words that come to mind when they think of the vocabulary word. For example, your student might think of *agreement* or *contract* when they think about the Mayflower Compact. These words might be easier to associate with a visual representation, such as a piece of paper with a signature on it than the vocabulary word itself.

Practice (Causes and Effects)

To assist in this activity, have your student create causes or effects of events that are already listed. It may be difficult for your student to think about a cause of an event, so have them work backward from the event to determine the cause.

Learning Styles

Auditory learners may enjoy having a discussion about the ways Indigenous people's lives changed as a result of the European settlers.

Visual learners may enjoy drawing their own map of the colonies and the different colonial regions.

Kinesthetic learners may enjoy acting out various colonial jobs, such as being a cooper or blacksmith.

Extension Activities

Virtual Field Trip

Look up the official websites for Jamestown, Plimoth Patuxet Museums, or another colonial settlement. Many of the websites have videos, simulations, and games your student can engage in to learn more about life in the colonies.

Tie-Dye Fun

One of the cash crops in the Southern Colonies was indigo. Indigo was often used to dye things blue. Look up recipes for natural dye or use store bought dye to help your student tie-dye some clothing. As they dye the cloth, discuss why indigo might have been such an important crop for people in Europe to have.

Answer Key

Practice *(Visualizing Vocabulary)*
Drawings will vary.

Practice *(New World Timeline)*
In order from left to right: D, A, B, E, C

Practice *(Causes and Effects)*
Answers will vary. Possible answers:

Cause: Cash crops like cotton and tobacco made the Southern Colonies a lot of money.
Effect: Indentured servants, and eventually slaves, were sent to the New World to work on plantations.

Cause: The Puritans had very strict laws.
Effect: When Puritans broke a law, they were punished and sometimes expelled from the colony.

Cause: Colonists relied on trading with others to provide what they needed.
Effect: Many colonists traveled on waterways to quickly get to faraway places to trade.

Quick Review

Refer to the statement your student circled in the Show What You Know section to self-assess their knowledge of the chapter concepts. Then to assist in determining if your student is ready to take the assessment, consider:

- Having your student sequence events that led to the development of colonies in the New World.
- Having your student identify differences between the different regions of colonies.

Discover! SOCIAL STUDIES • GRADE 4 • CHAPTER 1 ASSESSMENT

25

Chapter Assessment

Circle the correct word to complete each sentence.

1. _____ is making a fair trade without using money.

   A. Purchasing

   B. Bartering

   C. Native

2. Europeans, like Columbus, were hoping to find and trade _____ while exploring.

   A. journals

   B. maps

   C. spices

3. The _____ Time is the time period during the first winter in Jamestown when many people died.

   A. Spices

   B. Starving

   C. Indigenous

4. The need for more people to work on plantations that grew cash crops caused Europeans to send indentured servants and _____ to the Southern Colonies.

   A. slaves

   B. imports

   C. compacts

Circle the correct answer for each question.

5. Why did Columbus sail to the New World?

   A. to find a new trade route to Asia

   B. to trade with Indigenous people in the Caribbean

   C. to prove the world was round

6. Why did some Europeans want to settle in North America?

   A. to have their own land

   B. to start new lives

   C. to be rich

   D. all of the above

7. Why did the Pilgrims come to the New World?

   A. for religious freedom

   B. to be rich

   C. to grow cash crops

8. What is one way the Wampanoag people helped the Pilgrims?

   A. They gave them huge ships to sail back to England.

   B. They taught the Pilgrims how to grow and harvest crops.

   C. They taught them their religion.

9. What did the Mayflower Compact do?

   A. It set up a government for the Pilgrims that was led by the people.

   B. It made someone a king who was in charge of the people.

   C. It set up the head of the church as the leader.

10. How were the Puritans and Pilgrims different?

    A. The Pilgrims came from Africa and the Puritans came from Europe.

    B. The Puritans came better prepared to live in the New World than the Pilgrims.

    C. The Puritans relied on the Indigenous people for help, but the Pilgrims did not.

11. Which of the following sentences describes how colonists used waterways? Circle all correct answers.

    A. Colonists used fresh water from rivers for everyday needs such as drinking, bathing, and washing clothes.

    B. Rivers were used as pathways to get from one place to another.

    C. Colonists used rivers mostly for entertainment.

12. What cash crops were exported from the Southern Colonies to Europe?

    A. manufactured goods and beavers

    B. shellfish, lobster, and maple syrup

    C. tobacco, indigo, and cotton

Read each sentence. Circle True or False.

13. True or False The Mayflower Compact was the first example of democracy in the United States, and those democratic ideas are still present in our government today.

14. True or False Pilgrims thought land should be shared, while Indigenous people believed land was owned by individuals.

15. True or False The Pilgrims used metal tools and big ships, and the Indigenous people only used what they could make or get from nature.

16. True or False The populations of Indigenous people in the New World eventually decreased due to diseases being brought over by colonists.

17. True or False The original Thirteen Colonies were located on the west coast of the United States.

18. True or False Blacksmiths, coopers, and tailors were all jobs found in the colonies.

19. True or False Land around rivers provided moist, fertile soil for growing crops.

20. Order the events that led to the creation of the Jamestown settlement by numbering the statements below from 1 (first) to 4 (last).

_____ Settlers built a fort on the James River.

_____ Jamestown eventually became successful because they were able to grow and sell tobacco.

_____ A man named John Smith guided a group of people to Jamestown from England.

_____ During the first winter, many people died of starvation and disease.

21. Draw a line to match the colonial region to its description.

New England	Many colonists grew cash crops, such as tobacco, cotton, and indigo.
Middle Colonies	There were many forests. A lot of colonists became shipbuilders and fishermen.
Southern Colonies	Farmers grew wheat and grains, while other people started their own businesses.

28

Discover! SOCIAL STUDIES • GRADE 4 • CHAPTER 1 ASSESSMENT

Chapter Assessment Answer Key

1. B

2. C

3. B

4. A

5. A

6. D

7. A

8. B

9. A

10. B

11. A, B

12. C

13. True

14. False

15. True

16. True

17. False

18. True

19. True

20. 2: Settlers built a fort on the James River.

4: Jamestown eventually became successful because they were able to grow and sell tobacco.

1: A man named John Smith guided a group of people to Jamestown from England.

3: During the first winter, many people died of starvation and disease.

21.

New England	→	There were many forests. A lot of colonists became shipbuilders and fishermen.
Middle Colonies	→	Farmers grew wheat and grains, while other people started their own businesses.
Southern Colonies	→	Many colonists grew cash crops, such as tobacco, cotton, and indigo.

Alternative Assessment

Project: Brochure

Project Requirements or Steps:

A brochure is a short flyer or advertisement with information about a topic. For this project, create a brochure about the New World and Thirteen Colonies. Include the following information in your brochure:

- Title·
- Pictures or sketches
- Information about how the New World was "discovered"
- Descriptions of the first settlements in North America (Jamestown, Plymouth, and Massachusetts Bay)
- Descriptions of daily life in the different colonial regions (New England, Middle Colonies, and Southern Colonies)

Alternative Assessment Rubric

Use the following rubric to grade your student's assessment.

	4	3	2	1	Points
Creativity and Neatness	The brochure is creative and fun as well as neat and easy to follow.	The brochure is creative and fun, but it is a little hard to read or understand.	The brochure is not very creative, but it is very neat.	The brochure is not creative or neat.	
Quality of Content	The brochure contains a lot of high quality information that is both interesting and educational.	The brochure contains a lot of information, but it is fairly simple and straightforward.	The brochure contains a few facts, but it is not very educational or interesting.	The content of the brochure is not educational or interesting.	
Connections	The brochure makes clear and repetitive connections to the chapter.	The brochure is connected to the chapter.	The brochure is somewhat connected to the chapter.	The brochure is not connected to the chapter.	
Grammar and Mechanics	The brochure has no grammar issues and uses advanced vocabulary.	The brochure contains a few grammar mistakes and uses age-appropriate vocabulary.	The brochure contains several grammar mistakes and uses age-appropriate vocabulary.	The brochure contains a distracting number of grammar mistakes and uses overly simplified vocabulary.	

Total Points _____/16

Average _____

Discover! SOCIAL STUDIES • GRADE 4 • CHAPTER 1 ASSESSMENT

31

Lesson Objectives

By the end of this lesson, your student will be able to:

- identify the causes of the French and Indian War
- describe why the British wanted to gain land during the French and Indian War

Supporting Your Student

Explore

This section asks your student to think more deeply about an argument or conflict that they had with a sibling or a friend and how disagreeing on which movie to watch or game to play could have caused them to become upset or angry. You might try to have your student explain the circumstances of a specific disagreement, from how it began to how it was resolved, and how this type of disagreement might be similar to those that countries have. For example, fighting over a toy you want is in some ways similar to countries fighting over resources they need or want.

Read (The Ohio River Basin)

One way to help your student understand the frequent land disputes between France and England is to discuss the lack of clear dividing lines or boundaries between the land claimed by the French and the land claimed by the British. Since there were no established borders, British colonists could easily move onto land that the French claimed and begin using it for their benefit.

Many areas, especially the lands around the Ohio Valley and the Great Lakes, were disputed. The French felt that these lands were theirs because they had moved there first and had established trading posts. The British colonists felt that these lands were theirs because the English monarchy had given them the right to claim land from the east coast to the west coast. Over time, the disagreements over which country could or should control these lands led to the French and Indian War.

Learning Styles

Auditory learners may enjoy discussing why the Ohio River Basin was so important to the French, British,

and Indigenous peoples.

Visual learners may enjoy looking at maps online to see how the shapes of territories in North America changed from the 1600s to the 1800s. They might also enjoy creating an infographic to illustrate these changes over time.

Kinesthetic learners may enjoy pretending to be an Indigenous person who is trying to convince there tribe to join the French or the British. Have your student create a convincing argument using what they learned.

Extension Activities

Sports Rivalries

One way to help your student understand the competition between certain countries, especially rival countries, is to look at the rivalries that exist in sports competitions around the world. For example, football (or soccer) has intense rivalries between certain countries like Brazil and Argentina or Spain and Portugal. Competitions such as the Olympics, The World Cup, the Tour de France, and the World Rally Championship also have athletes from different countries competing against each other.

You might help your student to choose a specific competition or sport and research at least one of its well-known rivalries, the causes of it, and some of its significant events. Discussing this information and drawing some parallels between sports rivalries and colonization rivalries could help your student connect to and appreciate the reasons and motivations behind such rivalries more easily.

Fur Trade

If your student is interested in learning more about the fur trade, have them research answers to the following questions and design a presentation with their findings.

- Where did the fur trade take place?
- What were trading posts and where were they?
- How did people travel to trading posts?
- When did the fur trade take place and how long did it last?

- Who was involved in the fur trade?
- What kinds of furs were common and why?
- How were the animals trapped?
- What did Indigenous people want/get in exchange for furs?

Answer Key

Explore

Answers will vary. Possible answers: Countries could disagree about land ownership, use of the land's resources, or whose citizens got to live on that land. If the countries could not agree, it could lead to arguments between its citizens or even war between the two countries.

Practice

1. D
2. A
3. E
4. C
5. B

Show What You Know

2. Ohio
3. Indigenous
4. farming
5. expand
6. allies
7. British
8. Answers may vary. Possible answers: The French and Indian War started because the French and the British both wanted control of the land in the Ohio River Basin. The French and the British had tension between them for a long time and did not get along.
   Disputes between the two countries were common during the 1700s. Their rivalry may have led them to war faster than a conflict between two other groups.

Lesson Objectives

By the end of this lesson, your student will be able to:

- describe how the French and Indian War changed life in the colonies
- summarize the differences in which countries controlled parts of North American after the French and Indian War

Supporting Your Student

Explore

To help your student think about where great leaders come from, it could be useful to have them name a few people who they think are great leaders. They might name someone that they know, like a teacher, coach, or local community leader, or they might name a president, historical figure, or even a fictional character. Have your student choose two or three great leaders and brainstorm some qualities that they share. You might ask guiding questions, such as "What makes a leader great?," "How do great leaders inspire their followers?," "Why do people follow a great leader?," and "Why would you follow one of the great leaders that you named?" Questions such as these could get your student to think more deeply about the qualities and behaviors of great leaders and why people choose to follow certain leaders. It could also help your student to think about what made George Washington a great leader.

You might also ask some guiding questions to get your student thinking about how a leader can become a better leader by learning from their mistakes. You might provide an example of a time that you made a mistake and learned from it and try to get your student to do the same.

Write (Which countries controlled different parts of North America after the French and Indian War?)

To help your student with this question, direct them back to the map they created, as well as the text. Emphasize to your student that the only part of North America that France still controlled after the French and Indian War were some islands near Florida.

Additionally, help your student by asking them to describe the ownership of land from the point of the Mississippi River. They should be able to explain that the land east of the Mississippi River belonged to Britain, while the land west of the Mississippi River belonged to Spain.

Practice

To support your student during this activity, remind them to return to the map they created, as well as the text. Have your student describe who owned parts of the land on the map before the French and Indian War (France owned land west of colonies and Great Britain only owned the land where the colonies were located and part of Canada). Next, have your student describe who owned the land after the war based on their map. Guide them through this discussion by saying something like, "The eastern side is the right side of the map. All of this land belonged to Great Britain after the French and Indian War. Let's highlight this as one of the differences in the land after the war. France had to give up all its land in North America, except for a couple islands. Let's list that as a difference too."

Learning Styles

Auditory learners may enjoy listening to you describe the changes in land ownership that happened after the French and Indian War while referencing a US map.

Visual learners may enjoy looking at primary documents from the French and Indian War. These are sources created from firsthand perspectives, and many can be found online.

Kinesthetic learners may enjoy creating maps of before and after the French and Indian War using various materials around your house, such as clay, paint, and felt.

Extension Activities

The French and Indian War and the American Revolution

Although England won the French and Indian War, the long-term consequences of winning were very negative and helped to set the stage for the American

Revolution. Help your student use a search engine to find out how the combination of England's financial situation after the war, its decision to tax the colonists, France's desire for revenge, and the military experience gained by the colonists during the war set the stage for the American Revolution. You might ask your student some guiding questions to help them gain some insight into this information. For instance, you might ask:

- Was it unreasonable of England to tax the colonists since it had invested so much money in winning the war?
- Were the colonists wrong to fight for their independence from England?
- Do you think that things might have been different if England had not taken control of such a large section of North America after the war? For instance, if England had taken a smaller section of land and not taxed the colonists, do you think that they could have retained control of the colonies and avoided further conflict?

Treaties that Changed the World

There have been many treaties that have significantly changed the world, including the Congress of Vienna (1814-1815), which ended the Napoleonic Wars and reshaped Europe, and the Treaty of Versailles (1919), which ended World War I. Help your student to research one other important historical treaty and discuss how it reshaped or changed certain aspects of the world. You might also discuss which country or countries gained or lost things, such as territories, because of the treaty and how that reshaped the world.

Answer Key

Explore

Answers will vary. Possible answers: A leader becomes great through experience and learning from their mistakes. A strong leader must be a great communicator. They must be clear, honest, nice, and respectful. A good leader also makes decisions that are fair and helpful. They look out for others. Great leaders also inspire and motivate people.

Read (The End of the War)

The Mississippi River should be traced in blue. The land west of the river should be yellow and labeled "Spain". The land east of the river should be colored red and labeled "Great Britian."

Write (Which countries controlled different parts of North America after the French and Indian War?)

Answers may vary. Possible answers: Spain and Great Britain controlled most of the land in North America after the French and Indian War. Spain controlled the land west of the Mississippi River, and Great Britain controlled all of the land east of the Mississippi River. France had given up all of its land in North America in the Treaty of Paris agreement except for a couple of small islands in the Atlantic Ocean.

Results of the French and Indian War

Practice

Answers will vary. Possible answers:

Before the War	After the War
• France controlled the land west of the Mississippi River and in the Ohio River Basin. • France controlled parts of eastern Canada. • Indigenous people traded furs with the French.	• Spain controlled the land west of the Mississippi River. • Britain controlled all the land east of the Mississippi River after the war. • Indigenous people who fought with France were afraid the British would force them to leave their homes, so they tried attacking the British many times.

Show What You Know

1. B

2. B

3. A

4. A

5. C

Lesson Objectives

By the end of this lesson, your student will be able to:

- analyze why there was conflict between the colonies and Britain
- identify events that happened between the French and Indian War and the Boston Massacre

Supporting Your Student

Explore

This activity aims to introduce your student to the idea of taxes. If possible, you might peak their curiosity by taking them to a local store to buy a pack of gum. Point out the price on its label, and then take it to the cashier. The cashier will charge you more than the price on the label. Emphasize this to your student and ask them why they think there is a price difference. After hearing some of their ideas, tell them in the United States, people pay a sales tax on items they buy. This extra money on items goes to the government, and then the government pays for public services that everyone uses, such as police departments and public libraries. Your student might find it interesting to look up what the sales tax is in your area and how it differs from other states in the United States.

Read *(Tension Grows in the Colonies)*

Remind your student that *tension* means showing feelings of being worried, nervous, or upset. When two people have an argument or a disagreement, the atmosphere might be tense. You might ask your student to think of an example of a time when they were upset with someone else, such as a sibling or friend. Then you might ask some guided questions, such as "Why did you become upset with them?," "What happened that created some tension between the two of you?," and "How did you resolve the disagreement?" Those questions could help your student connect to the concept of tension and why the colonists were upset with Great Britain.

One way to try to help your student understand the perspective of both King George and the colonists is by listing the reasons that the Proclamation of 1763 was a good idea and why it was not a good idea. Doing so could help your student appreciate both perspectives of this issue. You might also point out that it was supposed to improve things in the colonies and prevent further conflict, but its results were the opposite.

Learning Styles

Auditory learners may enjoy listening to an audiobook about life in the colonies during the tense time after the French and Indian War.

Visual learners may enjoy creating a flowchart of how taxes are collected and used today.

Kinesthetic learners may enjoy playing a game of charades where they have to get the other players to guess different items that were taxed, such as sugar, playing cards, or tea.

Extension Activities

Primary Sources

Have your student analyze several primary sources, such as images and documents created firsthand during an event or time period from the 1760s. You might find newspaper articles, diary entries, political cartoons, or war paintings. Encourage your student to see if they can connect any of the primary sources to events from the lesson.

Build a Model

Have your student use toy blocks or materials around your home to build a model representing the Proclamation Line on top of a large map. The line should extend over the Appalachian Mountains, as indicated on the map in the lesson. Ask your student to write or talk about how each group of people might have felt about staying on their own side of the line. Ask your student to make connections to a time they were separated from a sibling or a friend during an argument.

Answer Key

Explore
Answers will vary. Possible answer: If there were no taxes, we might not have some of the things we need or enjoy, such as good roads or public libraries.

Practice
Drawings will vary, but may reflect the following:

King George passed a law called the Proclamation of 1763. He ordered colonists to stay east of the Proclamation Line that ran along the Appalachian Mountains, and Indigenous people to stay west of the line. To pay for the French and Indian War, King George began taxing colonists on goods they used every day, such as sugar, paper, glass, paint, and tea. Colonists did not think this was fair.

Show What You Know
1. 5: King George passed the Stamp Act, which taxed colonists on all papers in the colonies.
   1: Great Britain fought in the French and Indian War and won the land between the Mississippi River and the Appalachian Mountains.
   6: Conflict between the colonies and Britain grew as the Townshend Act was passed, placing a tax on glass, paint, and tea.
   3: King George passed a law called the Proclamation of 1763 that ordered colonists to stay east of the Appalachian Mountains and Indigenous people to stay west. This angered many colonists.
   2: As colonists moved west of the Appalachian Mountains, many conflicts arose between colonists and Indigenous people.
   4: To pay off his debt from the French and Indian War, King George began taxing colonists on goods they used every day with the Sugar Act.
2. False
3. False
4. True
5. False
6. False

Lesson Objectives

By the end of this lesson, your student will be able to:

- compare and contrast the different viewpoints of the Boston Massacre
- compare and contrast colonists' feelings about paying taxes to England
- summarize the different ways colonists reacted to England's laws in the colonies

Supporting Your Student

Explore

If your student is having trouble thinking of an example from their own experience, try to ask them some guided questions that are more generalized. For example, you might ask, "If two friends cannot agree on what game to play, what could they do to decide? What are some ways that they could come to an agreement?" You might also ask, "What might happen if they cannot agree? How might things get worse?" Doing so could help your student connect to the growing tensions in the colonies and understand why the disagreements became intense and eventually led to violence.

Write *(Summarize two different ways colonists reacted to England's laws in the colonies.)*

Ask your student to make connections related to the ways they react when they are upset or when they think something is unfair. Emphasize that reactions are effects that are caused by something upsetting.

When your student is ready to answer the question in the Write section, ask them to return to the text under the heading "Colonists React." If your student needs support finding evidence in the text to write about, show them how to read through this section and highlight important information that answers the question. Read the first paragraph aloud, emphasizing that boycotting is a reaction to England's laws that taxed goods in the colonies. By refusing to buy these products, the king was affected because his government, and many British merchants were not making as much money.

Encourage your student to continue reading the second paragraph to look for another way colonists reacted to England's laws. Stop them to emphasize the idea of protesting. Speaking out against taxes and their lack of representation in the British government convinced others that the taxes were unfair and that they needed to do something to stop the king.

Practice

Remind your student that viewpoints are different beliefs or opinions. Maybe their viewpoint is that gummy worms are the best ice cream topping, whereas you love hot fudge. Explain that people might also have different opinions about the same event. For example, one person may describe Fourth of July fireworks as fun and exciting, while another person sees them as scary or unnecessary. Ask your student to come up with a few other real-world examples of topics that might cause people to have different opinions before returning to this section.

In this activity, your student should compare the different viewpoints on topics such as taxes and the Boston Massacre. To start, have them return to the text under the heading "Different Opinions." Have them read different views on taxes. In the second paragraph, it says, "Many colonists believed the taxes were unfair because they did not have representation in England's government." Ask your student to highlight this detail, then ask them which section of the diagram it should go in. They should indicate that it goes under the colonist heading. Details in the text about taxes helping the British government to protect the colonies should go in the middle of the diagram since the text indicates that this was the belief of some colonists.

Learning Styles

Auditory learners may enjoy writing and reciting a song or poem about the Boston Massacre.

Visual learners may enjoy watching the TV series *Liberty Kids* online, which shows the events leading up to and including the Revolutionary War.

Kinesthetic learners may enjoy presenting a puppet show of the Boston Massacre, including telling the story from one perspective and then retelling from the other perspective.

Extension Activities

Role Playing

To help your student connect with the different perspectives of what happened in Boston, have them role play the part of a British soldier or of a British citizen still living in England. Ask them to think about what kind of ideas or opinions they might have about the event and why they would have those opinions. Doing so could help your student understand that the same event could be interpreted in very different ways by different people.

Propaganda

The posters and images that were created after the Boston Massacre are examples of propaganda in colonial days. Have your student research what propaganda is and how it appears in advertisements today. They may enjoy creating their own advertisement with elements of propaganda.

Answer Key

Explore

Answers will vary. Possible answers: Taking turns and talking about why something is their favorite. They might also say that they can agree to disagree because it is ok for different people to like different things, like foods.

Write *(Summarize two different ways colonists reacted to England's laws in the colonies.)*

Answers will vary. Possible answers: Colonists reacted in two major ways to England's laws in the colonies. First, they boycotted British goods. This means they refused to buy goods that were taxed by the king, such as sugar. Second, colonists protested taxes. They spoke out against them by convincing others that the taxes were unfair by chanting "no taxation without representation" and by refusing to pay taxes.

Practice

Answers will vary. Possible answers:

(Colonist Perspective) Some colonists believed taxes were unfair. Most colonists thought the Boston Massacre was a tragic event, and that British soldiers were to blame.

(Both) Some colonists and British individuals believed taxes helped the British government protect the colonies.

(British Perspective) The British believed taxes were necessary. The British perspective of the Incident on King Street was that colonists were threatening British soldiers. The deaths were accidents.

Show What You Know

1. A
2. B
3. C
4. A
5. B
6. A

Lesson Objectives

By the end of this lesson, your student will be able to:

- describe the Boston Tea Party and its results
- compare and contrast the Loyalists and Patriots
- summarize the reasons a colonist might choose to become a Loyalist or a Patriot

Supporting Your Student

Explore

If your student is having trouble thinking of situations in which they would need to get someone's attention, offer these ideas:

- You need to get your caregiver or teacher's attention urgently, but they are on a video chat meeting. Can you let the person know without disrupting the meeting?
- Your neighbor's dog has gotten loose, but they are driving their riding lawn mower and listening to something with headphones.
- You are playing with your sibling, but it is no longer fun and now you are getting upset. Your sibling does not understand that you are not having fun anymore and continues playing. How do you stop them?

Read *(Sons of Liberty Take Action)*

If boycotting is a challenging concept for your student, explore other successful boycotts in history, like the Montgomery Bus Boycott, the Delano Grape Strike and Boycott by the United Farm Workers, and the global boycotts of South Africa in opposition to apartheid.

It may be helpful to note that boycotts are not often successful and are very difficult to organize. But when they are successful, they can have a big impact—just ask Rosa Parks, Cesar Chavez, and Nelson Mandela!

Read *(A Closer Look: The Tea Act of 1773)*

Tea might not be the most relatable product to your student. Help them imagine the level of control Britain had on global trade by asking them to consider a restraint of something they like. For example, all of the cereal (or another type of food your student enjoys) that comes into the US must come through Canada. Canada decides the only cereal they will allow stores to buy is your student's least favorite. They could order their favorite cereal online easily from another country, but that would be illegal. How does that make them feel?

Learning Styles

Auditory learners may enjoy describing what happened during the Boston Tea Party in their own words, perhaps incorporating different sound effects like the tea splashing into the harbor or the Sons of Liberty whispering about their plans.

Visual learners may enjoy continuing to explore works of Revolutionary-era art or looking at portraits of important figures of the era, like the Founding Fathers. The National Archives and Smithsonian Institution offer tremendous resources.

Kinesthetic learners may enjoy completing the evaluation of concerns exercise in Show What You Know physically rather than in writing. Select two different physical movements to assign to the two choices of Loyalist or Patriot. Here are some ideas: standing/sitting, jumping/spinning, arms on head/arms in the air, or facing forward/facing backward.

Extension Activities

Self-Portrait Artist Study

Examine personal portraits painted by Loyalist artist John Singleton Copley and Patriot artist Charles William Peale. Have your student complete a self-portrait in the style of one of the two artists.

Shipping Study

American merchants during the Revolutionary period probably would have loved two-day shipping! Unfortunately, if their shipment of goods from the British East India Company was delayed (or destroyed, as in the case of the Boston Tea Party), a quick replacement was not a realistic possibility.

Have your student research typical travel times for merchant ships to travel from Britain to Boston Harbor. Have your student compare it to the speed at which warships could travel and explore the differences between a merchant ship and a naval frigate.

Answer Key

Explore

Answers will vary.

Practice

Possible facts included in the advertisement:

If your student chooses the Loyalist side, they might give reasons like wanting to avoid punishment from the government, wanting to protect their business as a merchant, disliking the behavior of the Patriots, attending an Anglican church with an influential minister, being a German immigrant and liking the king's heritage, or being an indentured servant who was promised freedom in exchange for loyalty.

If your student chooses the Patriot side, they may mention their commitment to the ideal of liberty, the poor governing of the colonies by the British government, that being charged taxes without representation in the government is invalid, or that the British government had too much control over their ability to trade freely.

Show What You Know

1. C

2. B

3. A

4. C

5. P

6. L

7. P

8. L

9. P

Lesson Objectives

By the end of this lesson, your student will be able to:

- summarize and evaluate the parts of the Declaration of Independence

Supporting Your Student

Explore

Help your student brainstorm times they have successfully persuaded someone to do something. You might ask questions to get them thinking, like, "Have you ever convinced a sibling or friend to play a game you wanted to play even though they didn't?," "Have you ever persuaded a sibling or friend to compromise on something they felt very strongly about?," and "Have you ever gotten your parents to give in to a request after giving a very good explanation of your view?"

Read

As your student reads about the Second Continental Congress and the signers of the Declaration of Independence, lead them in a discussion of things they consider to be worth risking one's life for and what the founders must have felt during this time period. Emphasize that signing the declaration meant a person could be accused of treason and could be punishable by death. This meant the signers of the Declaration of Independence were willing to risk their lives to obtain freedom for their fellow colonists.

Practice

Support your student in summarizing the sections of the Declaration of Independence by asking guiding questions about the general purpose of each section. For example, you might ask, "Why would the colonists make a list of complaints?" when discussing the Bill (List) of Grievances section. This can help your student to evaluate why this section was an important part of the declaration. In this case, it helped provide factual reasons for separation from Britain.

Learning Styles

Auditory learners may enjoy listening to the Declaration of Independence read aloud or doing a choral reading with you or another learner.

Visual learners may enjoy watching a video of a dramatic reading or reenactment of the Declaration of Independence being read.

Kinesthetic learners may enjoy manipulating a printed copy of the Declaration of Independence text by cutting it into the four sections. They can arrange the sections in order or read through one section at a time.

Extension Activities

Compare and Contrast

Explore the similarities and differences between the Magna Carta and the Declaration of Independence with your student. The founders needed to find a legal precedent for rightfully declaring independence to avoid their efforts from being denounced as outright treason. After you do your research, ask your student, "What do these documents have in common, and how do they differ?," "What is the relationship between the Magna Carta and the Declaration of Independence?," and "What inspiration did the founders take from the Magna Carta, and what changes were made?"

For further exploration, your student can make a Venn diagram to show the comparisons and contrasts they discover. To do this, they can draw two intersecting circles. In the space where the circles overlap, they can write the ways the Magna Carta and Declaration of Independence are the same. Then they can write the differences in each of the outer parts of the circles that do not overlap.

History, Imagination, and Empathy

It can be hard to relate to the events of history because they can feel so far removed from today's world. These events can become more real for learners by truly envisioning themselves in the shoes of historical figures and relating to their shared human experience.

Listen to the song "History Has Its Eyes on You" from the Broadway musical *Hamilton* with your student. Lin-Manuel Miranda's George Washington shares the accumulated wisdom of his years with a young Alexander Hamilton during the Revolutionary War, ultimately warning him to always keep in mind that history is always watching. This means that people years later will look back on what happened and form their own opinions and judgements.

After you listen with your student, ask them to consider what that knowledge and responsibility must have felt like for George Washington and the other founders. Guide your student to think about whether or not the signers of the Declaration of Independence knew how important their action would be today.

Have your student create a poster or multimedia presentation slide that depicts the legacy they would like to leave behind. What do they want to be known for?

Answer Key

Write *(Write one reason the colonies should stay loyal to Great Britain and one reason they should want independence.)*

Answers may vary. Possible reasons a colonist might favor independence: Britain treated the colonists unfairly, Britain taxed them without letting them have a say in their government, Britain controlled their economy and trade, the British Army treated many colonists poorly, colonists were forced to let British soldiers live in their homes

Answers may vary. Possible reasons a colonist might favor loyalty to Britain: It could be considered treason to do otherwise, no colony had attempted such a thing in the past, the British army greatly outnumbered the Continental armies, the colonies had little resources to wage a successful war

Practice

Answers may vary. Possible answers:

- Preamble: explains that the colonists were declaring independence and lists the reasons why, explains that people had a right to break away from government if the government was unfair

- Declaration of Natural Rights: lists rights that everyone has that cannot be take away such as life, liberty, and the pursuit of happiness

- Bill (List of Grievances): lists complaints about King George III, being taxed without having a voice in government, Britain controlling the colonies economy and trade, British troops being mean to colonists, colonists being forced to house British troops, colonists not being treated like British citizens

- Resolution of Independence: restates that the colonists are declaring independence, states that the colonists tried to reach an agreement with Britain but were refused

Write *(What is one reason you think representatives may have felt uncertain about declaring independence?)*

Answers may vary. Possible answers:

- Fearing revenge from Parliament, the King, and the British Army if the plan failed

- The citizens of their state may not have been interested in going to war for independence, or even happy with the way Britain was governing the colonies

- They may have thought they would look better to the government if they didn't sign the Declaration

- They may have wanted to protect their families from future punishment

Show What You Know
1. C
2. A
3. B
4. D

5. Possible answers: The Bill (List) of Grievances lists what King George III has done to ignore and disrespect the rights of the colonists. He was not upholding the law equally in the colonies and Britain, taxing the colonies heavily, not including the colonies in decisions regarding their governance, and allowed the British Army to occupy the colonies.

Major Revolutionary War Battles

Lesson Objectives

By the end of this lesson, your student will be able to:

- identify on a timeline major events that led to the British colonies' independence from England
- identify important battles of the Revolutionary War, including identifying who won the battle
- describe the Battle of Yorktown and its importance in ending the Revolutionary War

Supporting Your Student

Online Connection

This activity helps to give your student perspective and to visualize the events of Revolutionary War battles, but it also helps with metacognition (the process of thinking about thinking). This is an important academic and critical thinking skill. You might want to guide your student with some leading questions.

Before watching the video:

- What do you think the battlefield looked like?
- Where do you think observers and onlookers would be?
- Do you think the armies began firing on each other as soon as they saw each other, or was it more organized?
- How do you think commands were issued?

After watching the video:

- Did the reenactment match your imagination?
- What was similar?
- What was different?
- How did seeing the reenactment change the way you envision these battles?

Explore

It might help your student to visualize how far messages had to travel by looking at them on a map. If your student is interested, find Boston and Philadelphia on a map. Examine the distance. Notice the distance between New York City and Ticonderoga, where the major engagements were occurring that John Adams referenced in his letter. You might ask these questions:

- Even though Boston is slightly closer to Philadelphia than Ticonderoga, John Adams says James Warren is receiving news faster than he is. Why is that?
- What would it take to receive news quickly from that large of a distance?
- Do you think it would be difficult to get accurate information when messengers are the primary method of communication? Why or why not?

Take a Closer Look

If your student is interested in military history, they might be interested to learn more about the American sharpshooters and their success using guerilla warfare techniques against the British. Search for videos online that detail this information (including how sharpshooters greatly contributed to American victory).

Create

There are scanned copies of newspapers announcing and commenting on the events at Yorktown available online. Your student may be interested in seeing and reading some of them.

Learning Styles

Auditory learners may enjoy doing a partner reading of the battle descriptions.

Visual learners may enjoy identifying battle locations on a map.

Kinesthetic learners may enjoy making their own flash cards of the battles and dates to place in order.

Extension Activities

Mapmaking

Your student can research battle maps for any of the battles discussed in this lesson. Encourage your student to examine the battlefield map in reference to the current satellite maps of the area to see if the landscape has changed much over the years (many battlefield areas have turned into parks). Your student can then draw their own battlefield map.

Health & Wellness on the Battlefield

Your student may enjoy researching an aspect of life in the American army during the Revolutionary War, like what soldiers ate, how they traveled, or how they dealt with illness.

Answer Key

Explore

Answers will vary. Possible answer: You might not know where troops are moving or if another part of your army needs help fighting in a particular location.

Write (Which battle do you think was most important in the Revolutionary War? Why?)

Answers will vary. Possible answer: I think the Battle of Yorktown was the most important battle in the Revolutionary War because it ended the war and gave the colonies independence from Britain.

Practice

1. The Battle of Bunker Hill
2. The Siege of Charleston
3. The Battles of Saratoga
4. The Battle of Trenton
5. The Battles of Lexington & Concord
6. The Battle of Long Island
7. The Battle of Sullivan's Island
8. The Siege of Yorktown

Show What You Know

1. Patriots
2. British
3. Patriots
4. British
5. Patriots
6. Patriots
7. British
8. Patriot
9. Answers may vary. Possible answers:

    1. The British army had been run down and was exhausted.

    2. The alliance between France and America had become extremely well-organized and the British were surprised by the tactile attack.

Lesson Objectives

By the end of this lesson, your student will be able to:

- identify key people of the Revolutionary time period
- explain how elements of the United States flag design represent the 13 colonies
- identify Flag Day as a holiday celebrated in the United States

Supporting Your Student

Play

It might be helpful for your student to read speeches or letters by the important people in this lesson before writing a speech. Speeches and letters can be found through the Library of Congress and National Archives online.

Explore

If your student is having difficulty thinking of symbols, go on a symbols scavenger hunt around your house, classroom, or neighborhood to look for symbols to add to the list.

Read (Symbolism in the US Flag)

The vocabulary term *apocryphal* is a challenging word. Say the word aloud for your student, and have them repeat it. If your student is curious about apocryphal tales, here are a couple more you can share with them:

- The story of George Washington saying as a child, "I cannot tell a lie, I chopped down that cherry tree."
- Nathan Hale was a Continental Army spy. When on the scaffold awaiting execution after being captured, he supposedly said, "I only regret that I have but one life to lose for my country."
- Martha Washington once named a stray tomcat "Hamilton" after the Founding Father, as a way to tease him about being girl-crazy.
- Marquis de Lafayette gifted then-president John Quincy Adams (son of John Adams) with an alligator, which he kept in the East Room of the White House for two months.

Learning Styles

Auditory learners may enjoy doing a partner or choral read-aloud of the important people in the lesson.

Visual learners may enjoy looking up more pictures of the people listed in this lesson by doing an online image search. They might also enjoy comparing various paintings and drawings of the people, noting similarities and differences in how they were portrayed.

Kinesthetic learners may enjoy reenacting the events of one important Revolutionary War figure's life, like Molly Pitcher retrieving water for soldiers on the battlefield and taking over her husband's cannon.

Extension Activities

Be Your Own Betsy Ross!

Have your student recreate the original US flag by making a paper collage, painting, or sewing a small version out of felt or other material.

Other Noteworthy People

There are countless people who contributed to the founding of the United States during the time of the Revolutionary War. Have your student conduct research on another figure not listed in this lesson. Here are some suggestions:

- John Jay
- James Madison
- Angelica Schuyler Church
- Martha Washington
- John Paul Jones
- Ethan Allen
- Hercules Mulligan and the person he enslaved, Cato
- James Armistead Lafayette

Have your student write a report, record a video, or record a podcast that gives important facts about their chosen figure and explains their importance during this time period.

Answer Key

Explore

Answers will vary. Possible answers: The stripes represent the 13 colonies. The stars represent the 50 states.

Write *(Identify one person that you had never heard of before from this lesson, what you learned about them, and why you think they were important to the American Revolution.)*

Answers will vary. Possible answers: I was surprised to learn about Molly Pitcher because I did not know women handled cannons in battle during the Revolutionary War. I think she was important for her bravery and dedication to the Patriot cause.

Practice

Trading card pictures and facts will vary.

Show What You Know

1. Abigail Adams
2. Benedict Arnold
3. Samuel Adams
4. George Washington
5. Alexander Hamilton
6. Thomas Jefferson
7. John Adams
8. Molly Pitcher
9. Marquis de Lafayette
10. Benjamin Franklin
11. colonies
12. stars
13. Flag Day

Lesson Objectives

By the end of this lesson, your student will review the following big ideas from Chapter 2, "A New Country":

- France and Britain went to war over the Ohio River Valley. (Lesson 11)

- Having won the war, Britain gained a lot of land in North America while conditions improved for American colonists. Indigenous tribes who were aligned with France suffered after the war. (Lesson 12)

- The war was very expensive, and the British tried to make the colonists pay for it through multiple tax acts that the colonists did not like and pushed back against. (Lesson 13)

- Tensions over taxation without representation led to protests—one of the biggest being in Boston. Britain sent troops to control the protests, but that only made the tensions worse. This resulted in the Boston Massacre. (Lesson 14)

- The colonists largely grew tired of continued taxation, lack of governance, and military presence from Britain. The Boston Tea Party led to Britain passing the Intolerable Acts, starting the domino effect that began the Revolutionary War. (Lesson 15)

- The Declaration of Independence stated the colonies' desire to become independent from Britain. (Lesson 16)

- The Revolutionary War began with battles at Lexington & Concord and ended with General Cornwallis surrendering at Yorktown. (Lesson 17)

- Many notable people contributed in important ways to the fight for American independence. (Lesson 18)

Supporting Your Student

In the Real World

Help your student connect to a pen-pal soldier stationed overseas. Suggest that they look for information about what to write in their letter, as there are often helpful guidelines and tips.

Write *(Select an event below. In one or two sentences, speculate (imagine and guess) the outcome if the event happened differently.)*
Ask your student to describe each event to activate their prior learning. You can follow up by asking:

- What did this event accomplish? What was the outcome?

- What could have happened differently that might have affected the outcome?

- What would have potentially changed if the outcome had been different?

Practice *(Check the Temperature)*
Remind your student that there is not an exact right answer for this activity. As long as they are thinking critically about the ways that tensions between Britain and the colonists were rising and falling as well as how the events shaped that feeling, they are on the right track.

Learning Styles

Auditory learners may enjoy listening to the big ideas read aloud and then putting them into their own words.

Visual learners may enjoy making vocabulary flash cards to review from or creating a "mind map" to review the material in the chapter. A mind map would show the main topic in the center with small information about the topic surrounding it in picture or word form.

Kinesthetic learners may enjoy doing "Check the Temperature" through physical activity, like drawing the suns on the pavement with chalk and standing on the sun that matches the tension level for each event.

Extension Activities

KWL Chart

KWL charts are useful graphic organizers to help your student think about what they already know and where they want to go with their learning. Normally, there are three columns: What I Know, What I Want to Know, and What I Learned. We are going to make some slight changes to our chart.

For a chapter review, it is a good idea to make these columns: What I Know, What I Need to Review, and What I Want to Learn More About. Your student can complete their chart after they have completed the review as a way to "dump" all their knowledge before completing the assessment. This is a very useful study technique. It also helps guide their self-directed learning beyond the chapter. Here is what it looks like:

What I Know	What I Need to Review	What I Want to Learn More About

Event Puzzle Pieces

Write each major event in the chapter on an index card and mix them up. You can use these in a variety of ways:

- Have your student place the cards into a giant timeline in the correct order.
- Quiz them on the significance of each event.
- Have your student draw two cards and explain how the first led to the second.

Answer Key

Write *(Select an event below. In one or two sentences, speculate (imagine and guess) the outcome if the event happened differently.)*
Answers will vary. Possible answer: If the soldiers who fired on the colonists at the Boston Massacre had faced consequences for it, the British government may have been forced to take the colonists' demands to self-govern more seriously. They may have found a way to increase their participation in government.

Practice *(Visualizing Vocabulary)*
Answers will vary.

Practice *(Check the Temperature)*
Answers will vary. Possible answers:

Thermometer 1 (Low tension): Boycotts

Thermometer 2 (Mostly low tension): Intolerable Acts

Thermometer 3 (Medium tension): Boston Massacre

Thermometer 4 (Mostly high tension): Boston Tea Party

Thermometer 5 (High tension): Declaring Independence

Practice *(What's the Link?)*
1. They were both presidents of the United States.
2. Samuel Adams organized the Boston Tea Party.
3. Boycotts were the resistance colonists decided on to push back against the Sugar and Stamp Acts.
4. The First Continental Congress was called so the colonies could decide what to do in response to the Intolerable Acts.
5. They were married, and Abigail was John's most trusted advisor.
6. Certain rights are considered natural and God-given, and when they are not honored, the governed have the right to sever ties with the government. This is the basis for the Declaration of Independence.

Quick Review

Refer to the statement your student circled in the Show What You Know section to self-assess their knowledge of the chapter concepts. Then to assist in determining if your student is ready to take the assessment, consider:

- Having your student explain how the French and Indian War led to the Revolutionary War.
- Having your student name four important people from the Revolutionary War period.
- Having your student name two British victories and two Patriot victories from the Revolutionary War.

Discover! SOCIAL STUDIES • GRADE 4 • CHAPTER 2 ASSESSMENT

51

Chapter Assessment

Circle the correct answer for each question.

1. What land was fought over in the French and Indian War?

   A. Appalachian Forest Gorge

   B. Ohio River Valley

   C. Detroit Rock City

   D. Western Fur Expanse

2. What reasons did Indigenous tribes have to ally with either France or Britain?

   A. They had a good trade relationship with France.

   B. They wanted to be able to remain on their ancestral lands.

   C. They chose sides based on inter-tribal rivalries.

   D. All of the above

3. Which was not a reason Britain was interested in the Ohio River Valley?

   A. It had very fertile soil for farming.

   B. The colonies were growing and they needed to expand.

   C. They knew there was an emerald mine there.

   D. The fur trade was very profitable.

4. Which Act announced that Britain had the right to tax and make laws for the colonies?

   A. Stamp Act

   B. Sugar Act

   C. Declaratory Act

   D. Townshend Act

5. Who defended the soldiers that fired on colonists during the Boston Massacre in court?

   A. John Adams

   B. Alexander Hamilton

   C. John Jay

   D. Benjamin Franklin

6. How did some colonists react to British taxation?

   A. protests

   B. burning their hats in public

   C. boycotting taxed goods

   D. Both A and C

7. What solution did the First Continental Congress decide on to the Intolerable Acts?

   A. running rude comic strips of the king in colony newspapers

   B. boycotting British goods

   C. painting Loyalist doors blue

   D. kidnapping British soldiers

8. Which is not a section of the Declaration of Independence?

   A. Preamble

   B. Declaration of Rights

   C. Bill of Indictment

   D. Argument for Freedom

9. Which battle effectively ended the Revolutionary War?

   A. Saratoga

   B. Trenton

   C. Long Island

   D. Yorktown

10. This general and later president is known as the Father of Our Country.

   A. George Washington

   B. John Adams

   C. Marquis de Lafayette

   D. Benjamin Franklin

11. Place these battles in the order they occurred:

Yorktown; Saratoga; Bunker Hill; Sullivan's Island; Trenton; Lexington & Concord

1. ....

2. ....

3. ....

4. ....

5. ....

6. ....

Discover! SOCIAL STUDIES • GRADE 4 • CHAPTER 2 ASSESSMENT

53

Chapter Assessment Answer Key

1. B
2. D
3. C
4. C
5. A
6. D
7. B
8. D
9. D
10. A
11. 1. Lexington & Concord
    2. Bunker Hill
    3. Sullivan's Island
    4. Trenton
    5. Saratoga
    6. Yorktown

Alternative Assessment

Project: Create a Game

Project Requirements or Steps:

Create a board game in which the objective is to get from the French and Indian War to the surrender of Britain at Yorktown. The game objectives and play should incorporate the big ideas of Chapter 2.

Include the following elements in the game:

- Clear instructions for how to play
- Necessary game pieces such as a game board, cards, pieces, etc.
- Objectives or goals for the game
- Clear end or finish to the game

Discover! SOCIAL STUDIES • GRADE 4 • CHAPTER 2 ASSESSMENT

55

Alternative Assessment Rubric

Use the following rubric to grade your student's assessment.

	4	3	2	1	Points
Connection to the Chapter	The game is very related to the chapter.	The game is related to the chapter.	The game is somewhat related to the chapter.	The game is not related to the chapter.	
Directions	The directions clearly explain the objectives, purpose, and how to win. The directions are easy to follow.	The directions explain the objectives, purpose, and how to win. The directions are easy to follow.	The directions somewhat explain the objectives, purpose, and how to win. The directions are somewhat difficult to follow.	There are no directions.	
Neatness and Organization	The game is very organized and neat.	The game is organized and neat.	The game is somewhat organized and neat.	The game is not organized or neat.	
Creativity	The game is very creative and original.	The game is creative and original.	The game is somewhat creative.	The game is not creative or original.	

Total Points _____/16

Average _____

Lesson Objectives

By the end of this lesson, your student will be able to:

- describe the reason the Continental Congress wanted to create a plan for the country's government
- define the word *confederation* and relate it to the states in the new country
- identify the purpose of the Articles of Confederation
- summarize the problems with the Articles of Confederation
- explain why the Articles of Confederation did not give enough power to the federal government

Supporting Your Student

Explore

The purpose of this activity is to help your student make real-world connections. If your student struggles with imagining playing chess, you might name a different game they're more familiar with. Help your student understand how understanding the rules of a new game before playing helps everyone play the game fairly. In order for the game to be fun for everyone, clear expectations for playing fairly must be established. Often, if someone does not play the game fairly, they can be disqualified. Connect this idea to why having rules in a country is important. Ask guiding questions such as "What if adults didn't know the laws about speed limits before driving somewhere?" or "Why is it important to know that it is against the law to litter?"

Write *(Do you think the division of power between the state and federal governments was fair? Why or why not?)*

If your student has trouble identifying issues with the division of power between the state and federal governments, help them focus on what might be the problem with every state being able to write their own laws and what might happen if every state had a different kind of money. Ask your student what might happen if they went on vacation to another state that used different money.

Practice

For this activity, it might be helpful to start with a conversation about possible solutions to each problem. Let your student brainstorm freely, but keep them on topic by asking questions such as "How could the power be shared more equally with the federal government to fix this problem?"

Learning Styles

Auditory learners may enjoy listening to you read a copy of the actual Articles of Confederation to pick out the powers it gave to federal and state governments.

Visual learners may enjoy creating a poster with a visual representation of a balance with descriptions of the powers given to the states and the federal government. They could draw a balance scale and list the powers of each on the appropriate side of the scale.

Kinesthetic learners may enjoy taping each of the following questions around the room and walking to each one to discuss answers with you.

- Why did the Continental Congress want to create a plan for government for the country?
- What is the meaning of confederation, and how did it relate to the states in the new country?
- What was the purpose of the Articles of Confederation?
- What were the problems with the Articles of Confederation? Why were they problems?
- Explain why the Articles of Confederation did not give much power to the federal government.

Extension Activities

Create Your Own Articles of Confederation

Have your student write their own Articles of Confederation between the adults and children in your home. Which powers are given to the adults, and which are assigned to the children?

Cartoon Drawing

Have your student draw a cartoon depicting some of the problems with the Articles of Confederation.

Answer Key

Explore

Answers will vary. Possible answers:

- If my friend and I don't know the rules, we would not be able to play correctly.
- We would each make up our own rules so that we could each win.
- We might disagree on our made-up rules.
- The game would be difficult because we wouldn't know what we were supposed to do with the pieces or how to win the game. There would be no point in playing!
- It is more fun to play games when everyone knows the rules because it's more fair.
- When we know how to win, we can play competitively.
- One specific example would be: If some people didn't know the rules of soccer and they used their hands, the game wouldn't be fair. It wouldn't be fun to play if everyone played it differently.

Write *(Do you think this is a fair division of power between the state and federal governments? Why or why not?)*

Answers will vary. Possible answers:

- States should not have their own form of money because trading between the states would be difficult. The federal government should have the power to make one form of money that all states use.
- The federal government had very little power. If each state acted like its own mini-nation, they didn't really need to work together.
- The federal government had no power to tax the states within the United States. The federal government could not raise money to improve the nation.

Practice

Answers will vary. Possible answers:

Problem	Solution
Every state had different forms of money.	Congress (the federal government) should only be allowed to print money for every state.
Congress had no power to tax the colonies and collect money for improving and defending the nation.	Congress should have the ability to charge taxes as needed.
The states had too much power and became like "mini-nations" that didn't work together.	Power should be evenly divided between the federal and state governments with three branches of government that share responsibilities.

Show What You Know

1. Continental
2. confederation
3. B
4. A, C
5. Answers will vary. Possible answers: The states had a lot of power, while the federal government had very little. States could make and use their own money, so buying things from different states was difficult. The federal government couldn't collect taxes to pay for a military or to make improvements to the country. In the Articles of Confederation, there was only one branch of government which made laws. Colonists thought this would be good because it avoided giving too much power to one individual, such as the king, but responsibilities were not shared among different parts of the federal government.

Lesson Objectives

By the end of this lesson, your student will be able to:

- identify leaders who worked together to form the Constitution, including George Washington serving as chairman
- identify the importance of the Constitution in United States history
- describe a republic, including how much power is given to leaders and the involvement of citizens in choosing leaders

Supporting Your Student

Read (Writers of the Constitution)

While reading this section, help your student understand that drafting the Constitution was a process, much like the process of writing an essay. Students can think about how long each part of the writing process might take them. Also, point out that their audience, or people who are reading their paper, might just be a few people. The Constitution was such an important document that would be read by an entire country of people for hundreds of years. Explain that it was difficult to pass the Constitution because so many people shared their opinions on what should be included in it. Have your student think about how deciding on a game can be difficult when there are many opinions being shared. Combining many people's thoughts can help us make important decisions, like the ones that were made during the drafting of the Constitution.

Write (If you had a chance to interview George Washington, what questions would you ask him about the process of writing the Constitution?)

Have your student think about what the delegates discussed during the writing of the Constitution. Help them generate questions regarding the process of writing the Constitution they still do not understand. Your student should try to visualize what the days of writing the Constitution looked like so that they could come up with some questions. Help them think about what George Washington may have said if a

lot of people were disagreeing on important issues. Your student might wonder about how long they met for or if they were allowed to take breaks for lunch or snacks.

Practice

Help your student generate important facts or big ideas about the Constitution by emphasizing how the Constitution is still relevant today. For example, guide your student to see how the Constitution laid out the rules for the different branches or parts of the government that are still used today. Emphasize that the Constitution (and the Bill of Rights) guarantees rights and freedoms of citizens in the United States. These rights and freedoms are still applicable today.

Learning Styles

Auditory learners may enjoy creating a script for arguments made by each of the delegates during the writing of the Constitution. They can assign each family member or their friends a different role and act out the script.

Visual learners may enjoy creating a multimedia presentation using images and bullet points to summarize why the Constitution was important.

Kinesthetic learners may enjoy playing charades to act out the vocabulary words from the lesson to an adult or sibling at home.

Extension Activities

Create a Constitution

Have your student make their own constitution between siblings, friends, or a pet. What rights and responsibilities does each person or pet have?

Constitution Poster

Have your student make a poster summarizing why the Constitution is so important. They should Include pictures or drawings as well as important facts.

Answer Key

Explore
Answers may vary. Possible answer: I see a man standing in the front above everyone else. I think that gives him importance. I wonder how he was chosen to be the leader.

Write *(If you had a chance to interview George Washington what questions would you ask him about the process of writing the Constitution?)*
Answers will vary. Possible answers: Did you enjoy being the chairman during the drafting of the Constitution? How did you think power should be split up between the federal and state governments?

Practice
Answers will vary. Possible answers: The Constitution is so important because it gives us an outline for how the country should be organized to create a balance of power. It helped split up the power between the federal and state governments. It provides citizens with personal rights and responsibilities.

Show What You Know
1. B
2. A
3. D
4. C
5. B, C, E
6. Answers will vary. Possible answers: A republic is a form of government that allows citizens to choose its leaders. The words, "We the people," describe a republic because the people in a republic elect or vote for their leaders. People in the country can help decide how the government is run instead of just being told what to do.

Lesson Objectives

By the end of this lesson, your student will be able to:.

- describe the role of slavery in America during the latter part of the 18th century
- explain the Great Compromise and how slaves would be counted as part of the population

Supporting Your Student

This lesson explores topics that are difficult and often uncomfortable. Discussion will be the primary method of engagement in this lesson, given this difficulty. Kids are extraordinarily thoughtful, curious, and want to understand the truth of history—but how it is presented matters. Educational research shows that elementary students need to: A) learn key points about slavery and B) have those lessons include the resilience and resistance of oppressed people, as well as the work of allies who fought alongside enslaved people.

Researchers have found that much of the discomfort comes from enslaved people being presented as passively accepting their fate and society and the dominant culture being presented as entirely accepting of the practice of slavery. Children inherently possess a keen sense of justice and want to find the "helpers" when people are being mistreated. Even though this part of history is painful, it is also a testament to the fact that when evil is present in the world, there are brave people who fight against it. Lifting up those voices provides the context kids want and need in order to process this information.

Here are some additional online resources that provide guidance and insight for teaching slavery to children:

- "The Hard Part of Black History: How to Talk to Young Kids About Slavery" (Mount Tamalpais School)
- "It's Not So Black and White: Discussing Race and Racism in the Classroom" (Scholastic Teacher)
- Slavery and the Making of America (PBS)

Take a Closer Look (Petition Against Slavery)

The 1688 Germantown Petition is written in very old language and does mention adultery (though in the context of separating married couples and giving people away to others; e.g., an enslaved man's wife being given to another man—another enslaver).

Reading about this document will be more digestible for young students. For this and all additional research for this lesson, it would be best to explore the topics together, so you can discuss questions or uncertainties that arise.

Read (Slavery and the Economy of the Americas)

Here are some suggested discussion questions for this section:

- Even in slave states, enslavers were less common than those that did not enslave people. Since unpaid labor drove down the cost of goods, how would this actually hurt those farmers?
- Though there were fewer enslavers than those that did not enslave, enslavers had a lot of power and influence. How would wealth and having more available time affect the amount of influence they were able to have?

Read (Slavery Redefined)

This section describes very difficult ideas. Here are some discussion points/questions:

- Do you think Britain would have been able to hold onto (and grow) its power and influence in the world without the high taxes it charged its colonies around the world? What if it had to pay for the labor that produced the goods being taxed?
- How are indentured servitude and chattel slavery different? (Answer: Indentured servitude is for a fixed amount of time and doesn't deny the humanity of the person in servitude. Chattel slavery legally does not recognize the enslaved person as a human person.)
- What are you thinking/feeling about children being legally born into slavery?
- Do you understand how the Virginia slave code created a separate class of humans so that they wouldn't "count" as people with inalienable, God-given rights?

- How do you think the attempt to legally define people in separate ways will affect America long-term?

Read (Who Is Being Counted, and Who Is Being Represented?)

Here are some questions to help guide your conversation:

- What do you think of the compromise the states reached?
- The colonists were opposed to being taxed without having representation in Parliament. Does it make sense that they accepted counting people for representation when they could not vote and their interests were not represented?
- What effect did partially counting enslaved people have on the number of representatives on slave states? How would this affect votes on laws about slavery?

Learning Styles

Auditory learners may enjoy reading aloud the poems of Phillis Wheatley, an enslaved poet who published her works in the latter half of the 1700s.

Visual learners may enjoy seeing maps of the transatlantic slave trade to provide context.

Kinesthetic learners may enjoy making vocabulary flash cards to study from.

Extension Activities

Expressing Freedom

"What does the idea of freedom mean to you? When you feel the most free, what are you doing or experiencing?"

Help your student spend a few moments thinking about times when they felt the most free, and what that was like. When they are done exploring these ideas and experiences, have them create a work of art that expresses what freedom means to them.

Your student can paint, draw, do graphic design, sculpt with clay, or make a diorama in a shoebox. Choose the method that will best showcase what your student wants to express.

Recovered History

The organization Anti-Slavery International has a wonderful web resource called Recovered Histories that offers a huge collection of primary documents and sources that provide valuable context for the transatlantic slave trade. Because these are primary sources from the period, the language will be challenging. Help your student explore these resources together and discuss any that you find appropriate and meaningful for your student.

Answer Key

Show What You Know
Matching

1. H
2. J
3. F
4. C
5. D
6. A
7. B
8. I
9. G
10. E

Short Essay

The point of this essay is reflection, so use this as a starting point for further discussion as needed, rather than to quantify the number of facts mentioned. Notice how your student connects their thoughts and feelings to the content of the lesson and determine how well they have processed it. If there are areas that are lacking, review and discuss those sections further.

Lesson Objectives

By the end of this lesson, your student will be able to:

- describe the important ideas mentioned in the preamble to the Constitution
- identify the purposes of the Constitution

Supporting Your Student

Create

Your student may need help setting up their lift-the-flap graphic organizer. If they have experience using a crafting knife, you may suggest using that instead of scissors to cut the flaps (with supervision). If using scissors, they may benefit from a demonstration of getting the cuts started for the flaps.

You may want to remind your student to be mindful of the glue when placing the sheets together. If the glue spreads into the area under the flaps, it may be difficult to write on.

Read (What Comes Next?)

Your student may connect more deeply to information in this section with a guided discussion comparing the preambles of both the Declaration of Independence and the Constitution.

- Pause after reading "You might remember the term *preamble* from the Declaration of Independence." Activate their prior knowledge by asking what the purpose of that preamble was.
- After reading the preamble to the Constitution, ask your student to make connections between the two texts. They may note that they're both introductions, or that they both list the reasons for the documents they begin.

Read (Consider This)

Remind your student that the first purpose for the Constitution stated in the preamble is to form "a more perfect union." Here are some guided discussion questions that may provide additional context for your student:

- What did the founding fathers feel was imperfect about British governance in the colonies?
- What did the founding fathers think government should do?
- Do you think the British government enacting laws to punish the colonists for expressing their disagreements may have influenced how the colonists envisioned the new government?

Learning Styles

Auditory learners may enjoy listening to recordings of the preamble being read.

Visual learners may enjoy using colored pens to underline each of the six purposes listed in the preamble in a different color.

Kinesthetic learners may enjoy responding to Show What You Know through movement; i.e., standing for True and sitting for False.

Extension Activities

Preserving History

The National Archives offered a virtual field trip on Constitution Day in 2014. Watch the section of the field trip on the Rotunda for the Charters of Freedom with your student to see how these documents are displayed today.

Ask your student to explore the National Archives online to find out more about document preservation and what goes into keeping these treasured artifacts available for the public. Based on their findings, your student can make a list of 3-5 questions they have about the process, specific documents, or about being an archivist. Encourage your student to send their questions to the National Archives Museum.

Constitution Day

Your student can investigate the origins and current traditions surrounding Constitution Day in the United States. After they do their research, allow your student to choose between making a slideshow presentation about the holiday or planning an imaginary celebration for the holiday with events and a menu inspired by history.

Answer Key

Show What You Know

1. False
2. True
3. False
4. True
5. False
6. False
7. True
8. True
9. False
10. True

Lesson Objectives

By the end of this lesson, your student will be able to:

- compare and contrast how Anti-Federalists and Federalists viewed the Constitution
- identify what additions Anti-Federalists wanted to make to the Constitution
- describe the Bill of Rights as a document that was added to the Constitution stating freedoms granted to people

Supporting Your Student

In the Real World

Your student might not know much about local charities or have any idea how to get in touch with one. Help your student locate an organization they would be interested in by talking to them about the issues they care about and finding a non-profit that addresses those issues. This will deepen their connection to the activity and make it more personally meaningful.

For this activity, it would be best to reach out to the CEO, executive director, or board president.

Write *(Compare and contrast the views of the Federalists and Anti-Federalists in the Venn diagram below.)*

If your student is struggling to come up with things Federalists and Anti-Federalists have in common, you might ask these questions to get them thinking:

- Both sides seemed to feel very strongly about their opinion. Why do you think they cared so much?
- What were they trying to accomplish? What was their goal?
- What challenges did they face in getting what they wanted?

Write *(Select one of the amendments in the Bill of Rights that means a lot to you. Explain why you think it is important, and what you find most meaningful about it.)*

If your student struggles to identify the right they'd like to write about, discuss what each summary of the amendment means to them. Talk through real-life situations in which the amendments apply (e.g., we are able to express our opinions in public, even if we disagree with the government; the government cannot force you to let the military use your house; you can't be held in jail forever without being accused of a crime and standing trial; etc.).

Learning Styles

Auditory learners may enjoy doing a choral reading of the amendments in the Bill of Rights.

Visual learners may enjoy taking a virtual field trip that explores the writing and ratifying of the Constitution.

Kinesthetic learners may enjoy playing Amendments Charades to study the first 10 amendments.

Extension Activities

Amendment Memory Game

Your student can write the words *first* through *tenth* on 10 index cards. Then have them write the summary of the amendments in the Bill of Rights on 10 more. Mix up the cards and spread them out, writing-side down, on a table. They can play Memory by flipping over cards to match the correct pairs.

Evaluating Arguments

You and your student can examine summaries and explanations of some of *The Federalist Papers* essays (notable selections include 10, 51, and 70). Walk through the ideas presented in the essay summaries and encourage your student to determine the strengths and weaknesses in the argument.

Answer Key

Write *(Compare and contrast the views of the Federalists and Anti-Federalists in the Venn diagram below.)*

Answers will vary. Possible answers:

Federalists: favored a strong central federal government, wanted a strong executive, thought the Constitution didn't need amendments

Anti-Federalists: felt the states didn't have enough power, wanted individual rights guaranteed, didn't want a strong federal government or strong executive, feared having a government too much like what they'd just left

Both: want to steer the direction of the new nation, cared deeply about the future of the nation, had to reach an agreement between the states

Write *(Select one of the amendments in the Bill of Rights that means a lot to you. Explain why you think it is important, and what you find most meaningful about it.)*

Answers will vary depending on which amendment your student chooses.

Show What You Know

1. 3

2. 7

3. 8

4. 2

5. 6

6. 4

7. 10

8. 1

9. 9

10. 5

11. The order your student places the amendments in is not as important as their thought process in completing the activity. Once they are finished, have them explain their reasoning to ensure they've thought it through and spent time evaluating each amendment for its importance and relevance to their lives.

Lesson Objectives

By the end of this lesson, your student will be able to:

- summarize how the Constitution was adopted and ratified
- explain how leaders worked to educate people in their states about the Constitution so they would accept it
- describe more than one reason for the success of the Constitution

Supporting Your Student

Create

If your student is having trouble remembering which side each important person was on, use the material in Lesson 24 to give hints. Here are some examples:

- Thomas Jefferson: He was concerned about not having a Bill of Rights.
- Alexander Hamilton: He believed the Constitution was clear the way it was written.
- James Madison: He supported the Constitution, but he could also see some compromises needed to be made.

Explore

Help your student think of a time that they may have been frustrated by unclear or changing expectations by sharing a time that you have personally experienced this frustration. Think of a time that you understood the expectations to be one thing, but they turned out to be something else entirely or a time that someone changed the expectations or rules on you unexpectedly.

Read (Making Connections)

Deepen your students learning by asking these follow-up discussion questions:

- What do you think the Founding Fathers learned from having to change their plans about reconciling with Britain and then fighting for independence?
- How do you think this influenced their ability to change from the Articles of Confederation to an entirely new document for the structure of the United States government?

Play

Guide your student if they are in need of assistance in writing their paragraph to Rhode Island. Ask them to explain in their own words what the strengths of the Constitution are. Ask them what they think life would be like for Rhode Island if it didn't agree to be part of the United States, and why it would be better if it did.

Learning Styles

Auditory learners may enjoy listening to a reading of an essay from *The Federalist Papers*.

Visual learners may enjoy viewing the original Publius essays as they appeared in historical newspapers, viewable via the Library of Congress online.

Kinesthetic learners may enjoy making puppets to present arguments for or against the Constitution.

Extension Activities

Ratification Hopscotch

Have your student research the order in which the first nine states required to ratify the Constitution signed the document. Then, have them draw a hopscotch and label each square with the states in order. They can do the hopscotch until they can recite the nine states in order.

Founding Documents Scavenger Hunt

Have your student research who signed each of the four documents founding the United States (Declaration of Independence, Treaty of Alliance with France, Treaty of Paris, the Constitution). They should compare the list of signers until they can identify the one Founding Father who signed all four documents. (Answer: Benjamin Franklin)

Answer Key

Online Connection

Under the Articles of the Confederation, Congress could: pass laws, make treaties, declare war, maintain a military, coin money, establish a post office, conduct foreign business

Congress could not: enforce laws, collect taxes, establish federal courts, elect a president

Show What You Know

1. unanimously

2. nine

3. Publius

4. Alexander Hamilton, James Madison, John Jay

5. George Washington, Benjamin Franklin

6. Massachusetts Compromise

7. Bill of Rights

8. Answers may vary. Possible answers:

- The system of checks and balances creates clear boundaries and more equally distributed power between the three branches of government, which prevents any one part of the federal government becoming too powerful.

- The difficulty in amending the Constitution protects the document from political whims.

- The Bill of Rights protects what the United States considers to be fundamental basic rights that can never be violated by the government. These protections are what makes this a free country.

- The Constitution is the supreme law of the land, and no lesser law can contradict what is contained in the Constitution.

- This document affirms to the citizens of the United States and the rest of the world that a government can exist based entirely on the ideals of liberty and justice for all, even if the fulfillment of that promise has been a long and incomplete journey.

Lesson Objectives

By the end of this lesson, your student will review the following big ideas from Chapter 3.

- After independence from Britain, the Articles of Confederation was the first constitution of the United States, which was agreed on by the original 13 states to develop a new government system. (Lesson 20)

- The US Constitution is the most basic law of the United States. All other laws, including local, state, and federal laws, must agree with the US Constitution. (Lesson 21)

- The Great Compromise of 1787 created a two-house legislature: the Senate (upper house) and the House of Representatives (lower house). It also gave southern states the right to count slaves as three-fifths of a person to their populations. (Lesson 22)

- The US Constitution is a document established by the US government and is the supreme law of the land. It includes a preamble, which provides the rules for the structure and operation of the US government. (Lesson 23)

- At the Constitutional Convention, state delegates broke into two factions: Federalists, who favored a strong central government, and Anti-Federalists, who thought the Constitution gave the federal government too much power. (Lesson 24)

- The Constitution was a much stronger document than the Articles of Confederation, allowing the federal government to operate more functionally than before. (Lesson 25)

Supporting Your Student

Practice (*Visualizing Vocabulary*)

Help your student visualize important vocabulary by encouraging them to think of an image that is best associated with the word. To do this, it would be helpful to have your student look through images that are associated with the word. For example, when defining the words Bill of Rights, your student may think of the First Amendment to the United States, which is the freedom of speech and press, and to practice religion. Encourage your student to draw public speakers, cameras, or different religious symbols to denote the Bill of Rights.

Practice (*Venn Diagram*)

Help your student complete the Venn diagram by asking them to review the beliefs of Federalists and Anti-Federalists. They may do this by referring to the corresponding lesson on Federalists and Anti-Federalists or by using an online search engine to do research. If your student struggles with the middle section of the diagram, ask them, "Despite the differences between the Founding Fathers, what goal did they have in common?" To answer this question, encourage your student to research the similarities between Federalists and Anti-Federalists by using an online search engine. Your student may denote that the Founding Fathers believed that compromising was necessary to pass a constitution that favored both Federalist and Anti-Federalist principles. Federalists favored a strong central government (US Constitution) while Anti-Federalists favored individual rights (Bill of Rights). To compromise, a Constitution was created, which included the Bill of Rights.

Practice (*Timeline*)

Help your student create a timeline by asking them to review the worktext and identify the dates of the five key events in American history (listed in the practice section). Second, have your student identify the key features and accomplishments from each event. Then, ask your student to organize these key events in chronological order. For example, the earliest key event was the Second Continental Congress in 1775. Key events and accomplishments included the establishment of the Articles of Confederation, which was the first step in declaring independence from Britain. Encourage your student to fill out the rest of the timeline by following the same steps.

Learning Styles

Auditory learners may enjoy listening to an audio clip to hear the 52-word preamble written in the United States Constitution.

Visual learners may enjoy watching a documentary on the Great Compromise of 1787.

Kinesthetic learners may enjoy creating a book on the Bill of Rights by listing each of the first 10 amendments to the US Constitution on a sheet of paper. Encourage your student to draw or illustrate each amendment to reinforce important concepts.

Extension Activities

Preserving History

The National Archives in Washington, DC developed a virtual field trip on Constitution Day in 2014. In the collection of videos, watch the Rotunda segment with your student to see how these documents are displayed today. Then, ask your student to explore the National Archives website to find out more about document preservation, such as the Declaration of Independence, and how it is shown to the general public. Based on their findings, your student can make a list of three to five questions they have about the process, specific documents, or being an archivist. Encourage your student to send their questions to the National Archives Museum.

Failed Amendments

Throughout the history of the US Constitution, 27 changes have been made through the amendment process. Amendments are not easy to pass, and several amendments have been proposed over time. However, many amendments have failed to be ratified. With your student, research failed amendments in the United States, such as the Slavery Amendment, the Child Labor Amendment, and the Anti-Title Amendment by using an online search engine. Then, have your student create an infographic to describe the goals of each amendment, why it failed, and how many states are needed to ratify an amendment. Then, encourage your student to think about what may happen if these failed amendments were ratified and used today.

Answer Key

Practice *(Visualizing Vocabulary)*
Drawings vary. Ensure your student has the following definitions:

- Articles of Confederation: a document that outlined a plan for the American government and power that federal and state governments had
- Bill of Rights: a set of laws added to the US Constitution to protect citizens' rights
- checks and balances: the limits on each branch's power and how it can "check" the other branches if they overstep those limitations
- Federalist Papers: a series of 85 essays on the proposed new Constitution of the United States and on the nature of government in an effort to persuade New York state voters to support ratification
- Founding Fathers: the writers of the Constitution
- ratify: officially signing or certifying something
- US Constitution: a document that explains the rules and responsibilities of the government and how it should be run

Practice *(Venn Diagram)*
Answers may vary. Possible answers:

Federalists: favored a strong central federal government; wanted a strong executive; thought the Constitution didn't need amendments

Anti-Federalists: felt the states didn't have enough power; wanted individual rights guaranteed; didn't want a strong federal government or strong executive; feared having a government too much like what they had just left

Both: wanted to steer the direction of the new nation; cared deeply about the future of the nation; had to reach an agreement between the states

Practice *(Timeline)*

Answers may vary. Possible answers:

Second Continental Congress (1775): Establishment of the Articles of Confederation

Articles of Confederation (1777): the first constitution of the United States. This document officially established the government of the union of the 13 states. It also allowed Congress to raise an army, be able to create laws, and print money. It was weak because Congress could pass laws, but couldn't enforce states to follow them; Congress could not collect taxes. These factors made the government weak.

Great Compromise (1787): Convention used to write a new constitution, which strengthened the federal government and created the executive, judicial, and legislative branches. The legislative branches had two houses, known as the US Senate and US House of Representatives.

US Constitution (1789): Replaced the Articles of Confederation. With the help of the executive branch, Congress could pass laws and collect taxes.

Bill of Rights (1791): Part of the US Constitution that contains the first 10 amendments. The Bill of Rights was created by James Madison and provided individual rights.

Quick Review

Refer to the statement your student circled in the Show What You Know section to self-assess their knowledge of the chapter concepts. Then to assist in determining if your student is ready to take the assessment, consider:

- Having your student review the vocabulary words listed in the Practice section and look for the accuracy and quality of answers, including the clarity of definitions and sketches.
- Having your student discuss the beliefs of Federalists and Anti-Federalists and the value of compromise.
- Having your student describe the timeline of key events in American history, such as the ratification of the US Constitution and the creation of the Bill of Rights.

Chapter Assessment

Fill in the blanks using the vocabulary words in the Word Bank below.

Word Bank: Bill of Rights
chattel slavery
Founding Fathers
ratify
US Constitution
checks and balances

1. This document explains the rules and responsibilities of the government and how it should be run. It is known as the _____.

2. To make sure that each branch of government doesn't have too much power, the process of _____ was created.

3. During the Civil War, some slaves were owned, bought, and sold. This cruel form of ownership was called _____.

4. The Anti-Federalists supported a document called the _____, which gave citizens basic rights.

5. The writers of the Constitution were known as the _____.

6. States need to _____ a document before it can be used in American society.

7. What were some of the problems with the Articles of Confederation?

   ....

   ....

   ....

8. What was the purpose of The Great Compromise?

   ....

   ....

   ....

9. What were the six goals of the Constitution?

   ....

   ....

   ....

10. Who were the Federalists and Anti-Federalists? Why was compromise important?

    ....

    ....

    ....

Chapter Assessment Answer Key

1. US Constitution

2. checks and balances

3. chattel slavery

4. Bill of Rights

5. Founding Fathers

6. ratify

7. Answers may vary. Possible answers: America had a weak central government; The only branch of government was a Congress with one house; Congress had power over military and foreign affairs, but not over the affairs of each state; Congress could not enforce its powers or collect taxes.

8. Answers may vary. Possible answer: The Great Compromise of 1787 created a two-house legislature: the US Senate (upper house) and US House of Representatives (lower house). It also gave southern states the right to count enslaved people as three-fifths of a person to their populations.

9. Answers may vary. Possible answer: Form a new nation that improves the ideals of government, create a system of justice, preserve peace within the nation, provide defense for the nation at home and abroad, utilize federal spending for purposes of general national interest and benefit, and ensure that the promise of freedom is protected and lasting for future generations.

10. Answers may vary. Possible answer: The Federalists were Alexander Hamilton and John Adams. The Anti-Federalists were Thomas Jefferson and Patrick Henry. Compromise was important, because it supported Federalist and Anti-Federalist goals.

Alternative Assessment

Project: Infographic

Project Requirements or Steps:

You will create an infographic to show features of the United States Constitution. An infographic is a chart or diagram used to convey information or data quickly and clearly. Use the following steps to create your infographic.

1. Gather information about the features of the Articles of Confederation and the United States Constitution.

2. Create a title for your infographic related to the topic.

3. Include photos and drawings related to the topic.

4. Include information or data to explain and support the photos and drawings you included.

5. Include at least two similarities between the Articles of Confederation and the United States Constitution.

6. Present the information in a creative way.

Discover! SOCIAL STUDIES • GRADE 4 • CHAPTER 3 ASSESSMENT

75

Alternative Assessment Rubric

Use the following rubric to grade your student's assessment.

	4	3	2	1	Points
Connection to the Chapter	The infographic is clearly connected to the chapter.	The infographic is connected to the chapter.	The infographic is somewhat connected to the chapter.	The infographic is not connected to the chapter.	
Creativity	The infographic is very creative and aesthetically appealing.	The infographic is creative and aesthetically appealing.	The infographic is somewhat creative and aesthetically appealing.	The infographic is not creative or aesthetically appealing.	
Information	The information or data is very accurate and easy to follow.	The information or data is accurate.	The information or data is somewhat accurate.	The information or data is not accurate.	
Grammar and Mechanics	There are no grammar and punctuation mistakes.	There are one or two grammar and punctuation mistakes.	There are several grammar and punctuation mistakes.	There are a distracting number of grammar and punctuation mistakes.	

Total Points _____/16

Average _____

76

Discover! SOCIAL STUDIES • GRADE 4 • CHAPTER 3 ASSESSMENT

Lesson Objectives

By the end of this lesson, your student will be able to:

- describe the process that was followed to choose the first president
- identify how long the president now remains in office
- describe reasons why George Washington is known as the father of our country
- describe the role important leaders played in our nation's founding

Supporting Your Student

Read (The US Founding Fathers)

It may be helpful for students to create a table of the founding fathers to reference throughout the lesson.

Write (What are two reasons George Washington is known as the father of our nation?)

Have your student highlight the text with the answer. Encourage your student to write it out in their own words.

Read (Becoming the First President)

It may be helpful as your student reads to have them restate in their own words how a president wins the election. "In most cases, whoever gets the popular vote for that state wins all the electors in that state." Be sure to emphasize that candidates need the Electoral College to win the whole election. They win it by earning the popular vote in each state, which is allotted a certain number of electors.

Practice

Before starting, look at the map together. Ask your student what they notice about the map.

Learning Styles

Auditory learners may enjoy listening to a read aloud from a section of the Constitution or Federalist Papers. They may enjoy discussing the process for becoming the president.

Visual learners may enjoy seeing other political cartoons of the time, watching videos about the different leaders in the founding of our nation, or they may enjoy creating an infographic on becoming president.

Kinesthetic learners may enjoy highlighting key vocabulary and phrases or acting out being one of the leaders like Alexander Hamilton to persuade states to ratify the Constitution.

Extension Activities

Compare and Contrast

Print out recent election results from the Electoral College, and compare them to the 1788–1789 election. Your student can see how the Electoral College grew as the United States grew. Some similarities are that both times (present and 1778 to 1789) used the Electoral College. Also, some states maintained larger populations. For example, in 1789, Pennsylvania had a large majority of the electors with 10. They currently have a large number with 20 electors. Some differences could be the number of states and the number of electors per state.

Elections

Have a family election. Have your student create two choices, perhaps what movie to watch. Then have a voting booth such as an empty tissue box and paper ballots for family members to write their choices on.

Answer Key

Write *(What is an elector? What is the number of electors for a state based on?)*

Answers will vary. Possible answers: An elector is a person who votes in the presidential election. Electors are based on the state's population size.

Write *(How does a presidential candidate win the electors in the electoral college?)*

Answers will vary. Possible answers: To win the Electoral College for a state, you need the popular vote and you get that state's electors.

Practice

California has 55 electors, which is the most. Alaska, Delaware, Montana, North Dakota, South Dakota, Vermont, Washington, DC, and Wyoming have the least, with 3 electors. To win the presidency, you need to win 270 electors. Oregon has 7 electors, and Florida has 29 electors. The number of electors is based on the size of the state's population. To win the state, you must have the most votes in the popular vote for that state.

Show What you Know

1. False
2. True
3. True
4. C
5. A

Lesson Objectives

By the end of this lesson, your student will be able to:

- identify the branches of government
- identify the leader of the executive branch of government
- describe the president's cabinet and their responsibilities

Supporting Your Student

Explore

This activity is to get the student thinking about some of the people who are involved with running a country and their individual responsibilities. One way to help your student is to begin by discussing whether they would want to be a king, queen, or president and why they made that choice. Depending on what they chose, you might ask them, "Why would it be better to be a king or queen than to be a president?" Discuss the picture that your student drew and have them explain some of its details, such as the clothes that they are wearing, or the room or setting that is depicted in the picture. You could ask your student to explain why their country would need certain laws and/or why those laws would be useful or beneficial to the country. These prompts could help your student to complete this activity effectively.

Read (The Three Branches)

Ahead of time, you may want to read over this part of the lesson to brush up on your knowledge of the three branches of government in the United States. Keep it simple. Your student doesn't need to know everything about each branch, just the basics. Previewing the chart or going over it with your student will help. It is designed to be easy and quick to read.

Read (The Executive Branch)

This section focuses specifically on the executive branch, what the US presidents' responsibilities are and who specifically helps him. This is where the previous activities can really help your student. Ask questions like, "Do you think the Founding Fathers wanted the president to be in charge of everything?

Would it be a good idea for only one person to be in charge of running a country? Could a store manager run every department in the store?" These questions will help your student make connections between the problems that were experienced with the Articles of Confederation.

Practice

This activity is to see what your student has learned by placing the word bank words into the correct section. If they are having a difficult time, encourage them to go back to the lesson to see if they can find the answers.

Learning Styles

Auditory learners may enjoy debating what makes a good and bad leader or why it is or is not important to have rules.

Visual learners may enjoy creating an infographic that describes what the executive branch of the US government is, the different individuals who comprise the executive branch, and what their responsibilities are.

Kinesthetic learners may enjoy acting out through a skit or play in which your student and others recreate what happened at the Philadelphia Convention. It could be with either family members, friends, stuffed animals, or action figures. Your student could write their own short skit first and then act it out.

Extension Activities

Flash Card Practice

You can help your student create flash cards of the vocabulary words or of different aspects of the lesson, such as the different branches of the US government and their responsibilities. You could then use the flash cards to help your student connect to and benefit from the lesson.

Current Cabinet Members Video

You can help your student find videos using a search engine. These videos should be connected to the lesson and be about the different cabinet members and who they are, and what their specific departments and responsibilities are. Then your student could discuss what they learned about each cabinet member.

Answer Key

Explore

Answers will vary. Possible answer: The leader of my country is Joe Biden. The people who help Joe Biden are the members of his cabinet. If I became a leader of a country, I would plan some laws. I would call my country "Peaceland" because I would want it to have a lot of peace there. I would be the president.

Write *(Write down who oversees education and why you think this is an important job.)*

The Secretary of Education is in charge of education. Answers will vary about its importance, but it could include that the Secretary of Education makes sure that the students are learning appropriately, and the Secretary of Education is providing money to the states for the education in their state.

Practice

Legislative: congress, senate, makes laws

Executive: president, vice president, signs and vetoes laws, cabinet members

Judicial: supreme court, examines laws, nominated by president

Show What You Know

1. D
2. F
3. B
4. E
5. C
6. A

Lesson Objectives

By the end of this lesson, your student will be able to:

- identify the branches of government
- describe the role of Congress (Senate and House of Representatives) in making laws
- recognize the process a law goes through as it moves between the three branches of government

Supporting Your Student

In the Real World

During this initial activity, help your student identify the rules they must follow in different situations. There are family rules and rules that we must follow because they are laws adopted by the city, state, or country. How are these rules similar? No matter where these rules are enforced, they were all created to help prevent potential problems. Encourage your student to identify the reasoning behind rules they identify. Ask your student whether they know who created the laws they identify.

Explore

During this activity, your student will understand that rules make games easier to play and more fun. They prevent disagreements and misunderstandings. Ask your student how they felt when there were no rules in the game or when they disagreed with another player about the rules. Help your student relate this to real life. Explain that people in real life may disagree with the rules, but having a set of rules that apply to everyone prevents disagreements just as they do in a game. Throughout the lesson, you can practice this idea and encourage students to make more connections by playing a game without rules for a few minutes. Follow-up after these disorganized explorations by relating the feelings and frustrations to the real world.

Read (Legislative Branch)

With so much academic vocabulary, it may be beneficial to review the branches of government, titles of members, and jobs they employ before each day's work. Encourage your student to use the correct names for the branches and utilize resources such as the worktext as tools to help them remember. Students can keep flashcards, or a diagram, of the branches of government on hand for reference.

Learning Styles

Auditory learners may enjoy debating a law or rule with you, a friend, or family member. Remind your student that members of the government must be able to listen to each other.

Visual learners may enjoy drawing a sign to symbolize an important house rule. Post the sign somewhere in your home where all can see it. Have your student create a diagram of the three branches of government to help practice vocabulary and reinforce concepts. Have your student create flash cards to use in practicing vocabulary words

Kinesthetic learners may enjoy acting out their favorite rules or laws and filming it. Then they could play the video for their family or friends! Switch roles with your student for fifteen minutes. Your student can become the teacher and use flashcards he or she makes to quiz you or other family members.

Extension Activities

Law Charades

Using index cards, have your student write down the laws they know. Shuffle and turn the cards over. One person from a team chooses a card and acts out the card. Their team members or the other person playing tries to guess the law they are acting out.

Write to Your Senator or Representative

If your student is especially interested in a particular law or the need for a law, research the names of your senators and representatives. Write or type a letter explaining your views and hopes for change.

Answer Key

In the Real World
Answers will vary.

Take a Closer Look (Reasons for Rules)
Answers will vary. Possible answers: The "Do Not Enter" sign reminds people to stay out of an area. This rule prevents people from getting injured or injuring others.

Write (What problems do you feel your lawmakers should help fix?)
Answers will vary.

Write (Why do you think so many people must agree on a bill before it becomes a law?)
Answers will vary. Possible answer: If a large number or majority of elected officials agree upon a bill, there is a greater likelihood that a majority of citizens will agree with it as well.

Practice
Empty Box 1: Senators discuss and research the bill in a committee.

Empty Box 2: The House of Representatives votes on the bill.

Empty Box 3: The President signs the bill into law.

Show What You Know
1. The Legislative Branch makes new laws.
2. D
3. False
4. 6: The President reads and signs the idea into law
   1: A senator writes and shares an idea for a law
   4: The potential law is sent to the House of Representatives
   2: A Senate committee researches and discusses the senator's idea
   3: The Senate votes on the idea
   5: The House of Representatives votes on the idea

Take a Closer Look (Checks and Balances)
Answers will vary. Possible answers: The President is one person, so if two-thirds of Congress agrees that a law would benefit the country, chances are the majority of Americans feel the same way. This two-thirds vote gives a large number of elected officials the ability to challenge the will of one person, the President, for the good of the nation. Our constitution provides checks and balances that ensure no one person or branch will hold too much power.

Lesson Objectives

By the end of this lesson, your student will be able to:

- recall the branches of government
- describe the purpose of the judicial branch
- evaluate the importance of judicial review

Supporting Your Student

Read (Branches of Government)

As your student reads this section of the worktext, it may be helpful to use an online search engine to find videos on the branches of government in the United States. To help your student highlight the different roles and duties of each governmental branch, have them create a list of key differences. For example, the executive branch is responsible for *signing* and *enforcing* laws, the legislative branch is responsible for *creating* laws, and the judicial branch is responsible for *deciding* if a law is constitutional. Then, encourage your student to list any other roles and duties each branch may have, such as Congress's ability to declare war.

Read (Judicial Branch)

To better understand how judicial review is used, it may be helpful for your student to review how a bill becomes a law. To do this, use an online search engine and pull up a diagram, such as a flow chart, to visualize the steps needed for a bill to become a law. Then ask your student to identify where in the process judicial review would be used. Also, encourage your student to evaluate the importance of judicial review by asking them what would happen if the process didn't exist and/or how it would impact checks and balances.

Practice (Table)

Help your student complete the table by asking them to refer to the worktext. Then ask your student to identify who makes up each branch in the government by completing the second column of the table. For example, the executive branch is made up of the president, vice president, and Cabinet. Encourage your student to complete the last column by identifying the specific roles and duties of each

branch. For example, in the executive branch, the president is responsible for *signing* and *enforcing* laws. The president can also *veto* bills and *nominate* federal judges or Supreme Court justices.

Learning Styles

Auditory learners may enjoy recording a podcast to describe the features of the three branches of government in the United States.

Visual learners may enjoy writing a bill by proposing different ideas that can help people and the environment, such as planting more trees, creating universal health care, lowering taxes, or protecting animals from being killed for their hide. A bill should focus on a specific topic. If your student has two distinct proposals, encourage them to write two separate bills.

Kinesthetic learners may enjoy creating a song that features the three branches of government.

Extension Activities

Judicial Comic Strip or Illustration

Using an online search engine, have your student research as much as they can about famous Supreme Court cases, such as *Marbury v. Madison* (1803), *Schenck v. United States* (1919), *Brown v. Board of Education* (1954), *Tinker v. Des Moines* (1969), *Roe v. Wade* (1973), and *Regents of the University of California v. Bakke* (1978). Your student should understand:

- The premise of the case
- The perspectives on both sides of the argument
- How the case was resolved by the Supreme Court
- Social and political implications of the decision

Then have your student create a comic strip or illustration depicting what they think are the most important features of the case and what they've learned about it.

Role Play Interview

Conduct an interview with your student. First, have your student research the specific duties of the individual they wish to role play, such as a president, member of Congress, or Supreme Court justice, by using an online search engine. Then ask your student to think about some of the benefits and challenges that these individuals may experience. For example, if your student is interested in role-playing a Supreme Court justice, one of the benefits of being a Supreme Court justice is making a positive and lasting impact in society. One of the challenges a Supreme Court justice might face is deciding if a law is legal. Then, help your student conduct and record an interview about their experiences as a Supreme Court justice. Some of the questions you may ask your student include:

- What are some of the benefits and challenges of being a Supreme Court justice?
- What makes a law legal?
- What do you think are the qualities that make a good Supreme Court justice?

Answer Key

Write *(What are some of the duties of the executive, legislative, and judicial branches?)*
Answers will vary. Possible answers: Executive—president signs and enforces laws, can veto bills, chooses federal judges and Supreme Court justices; vice president counsels the president; Cabinet members advise the president on topics, such as climate change, wars, education, and health care; Legislative—creates laws; declares wars; can impeach the president for any wrongdoing; Judicial—decides if laws are constitutional.

Write *(What is judicial review and why is it important?)*
Answers will vary. Possible answers: The process of deciding whether a law is constitutional is known as judicial review. It is important to ensure that laws are legal and don't break the rules of the Constitution.

Practice
Answers will vary. Possible answers:

Branches of Government	Who Makes Up Each Branch?	Specific Roles or Duties?
Executive	President, vice president, and the Cabinet	President: Signs and enforces laws, vetoes bills, chooses federal judges and Supreme Court justices
Legislative	Congress: House of Representatives and the Senate	Creates laws, declares war, can impeach the president for any wrongdoing
Judicial	Federal judges and Supreme Court justices	Decides if laws are constitutional

Show What You Know
1. B   **2.** C   **3.** A   **4.** C   **5.** C

6. Answers will vary. Possible answers: Ruby Bridges was a child activist and the first Black child to attend an all-White elementary school in the 1950s. When she was six years old, she fought against racism and segregation. Segregation means to be separated by race, or the color of someone's skin. During this time, Black students were treated unfairly by attending separate schools, drinking from different water fountains and eating in different restaurants. While the Supreme Court ruled in 1954 that schools should not be segregated and made it clear that everyone deserves a good education, it took many years before the ruling was enforced. This impacted society, because it began the Civil Rights movement, where Black people fought against unfair and cruel treatment.

Lesson Objectives

By the end of this lesson, your student will be able to:

- identify how democratization has affected American life
- summarize how people are a part of the political process in the United States

Supporting Your Student

Write (How can democracy affect American life?)

Help your student answer this question by reviewing the basic principles of democracy, such as the freedoms to vote, speak, and practice religion. Then ask your student how these basic principles can affect American life. For example, your student may answer that the freedoms to vote and speak give people equal opportunities to make an impact in society, such as deciding who the next president should be. Encourage your student to also draw answers from their personal experiences, such as being able to vote for class president or a new name for a class pet. Then ask your student why these individual rights are important.

Read (Forms of Democracy)

As your student reads through this section in the worktext, it may be helpful to give additional examples of *direct* and *indirect* democracies. For example, offer your student a referendum by asking them to vote yes or no on basic questions, such as "Should students in class get pizza on Fridays?" or "Should people be fined for not recycling?" Then explain to your student why this is an example of a direct democracy and how it is effective for smaller communities. To help your student better grasp the principles of an indirect democracy, encourage your student to research any issues, such as air or water pollution, within their local community by using an online search engine. Then walk them through the process of contacting local elected representatives, their roles, and what they can do for the community. Inform your student that this process is an example of an indirect democracy, whereby elected representatives, not citizens, make laws that impact the community.

Practice

Help your student complete this table by asking them to review the worktext. Then ask your student to focus on one column at a time. For example, your student may state that "A direct democracy features all people who come together to make decisions and laws" in the second column. In the third column, your student may state that "A direct democracy affects American life by giving people the freedom to make decisions, such as answering a referendum."

Learning Styles

Auditory learners may enjoy recording a podcast to explain what democracy is, how it works, and its effects on American life.

Visual learners may enjoy watching videos on the origins of democracy and how they contributed to the development of American democracy.

Kinesthetic learners may enjoy creating an infographic on the basic principles of democracy.

Extension Activities

Vision Board

Inform your student that there are many ways to be an active participant in government and have a voice in society, such as volunteering in a soup kitchen, helping a classmate pick up plastic in the environment, or coming up with ideas to protect endangered animals. With your student, think about different ways you can help your community. Then encourage your student to visualize this process by creating a vision board that includes pictures and ideas. For example, if your student wants to protect endangered sea turtles, they can use an online search engine to find photos or draw sea turtles to add to their vision board. Your student may also list ideas that could help protect sea turtles, such as removing litter from the ocean that may harm sea turtles.

Design a Holiday

Ask your student to create a national holiday that celebrates democracy. Encourage your student to be creative and describe any food, games, or activities (e.g., fireworks) that may be used to celebrate the holiday. Also ask your student which day of the year the holiday should be celebrated. Then encourage your student to think about what the concept of democracy means to citizens and why democracy should be celebrated. Have your student share their ideas by creating an online presentation or poster.

Answer Key

Explore

Answers will vary. Possible answers: Voting is important because it gives people the opportunity to make decisions, participate in democracy, and support government leaders. Voting affects people in society because elected leaders have different ideas, beliefs, and priorities. For example, if members of Congress do not support climate change, then they likely will not create bills that help protect the environment.

Write (*How can democracy affect American life?*)

Answers will vary. Possible answers: Democracy places limitations on how long a person can serve in the government. Presidents can only serve eight years in total, giving citizens a chance to reelect or replace a president. It gives people the freedom to speak and make decisions. It gives citizens the right to have free and fair elections.

Write (*How do people play a role in direct and indirect democracies?*)

Answers will vary. Possible answers: In a direct democracy, all voters come together to make decisions and laws. They also vote by using a referendum. In an indirect democracy, people elect representatives to speak for them. People cannot create laws directly.

Practice

Answers will vary. Possible answers:

Forms of Democracy	Features	How American Life Is Affected
Direct	All voters come together to make decisions and laws. Voting is done by using a referendum.	People have the freedom to speak and make decisions.
Indirect	People elect representatives to speak for them. People cannot create laws directly.	People have the right to have free and fair elections.

Show What You Know

1. A, B
2. B
3. A
4. Answers will vary. Possible answers: A referendum is a special type of voting where people vote yes or no to changing a rule. A referendum can affect American life by allowing people in small communities to make quick decisions. For example, people can vote yes or no to building more parks, restaurants, or hospitals.

Lesson Objectives

By the end of this lesson, your student will review the following big ideas from Chapter 4:

- To become president of the United States, a person must win the Electoral College, which is a system of officials that chooses the president, such as George Washington. (Lesson 27)
- The executive, legislative, and judicial branches make up the three branches of the United States government. The executive branch is responsible for signing and enforcing laws. (Lesson 28)
- The legislative branch creates new laws from bills. Bills must be approved by Congress and the president of the United States before they become laws. (Lesson 29)
- The judicial branch interprets and decides if laws are constitutional or legal. The judicial branch includes federal judges and US Supreme Court justices. (Lesson 30)
- Democracy gives citizens the freedom to speak and make decisions. They also give people the right to have free and fair elections. (Lesson 31)

Supporting Your Student

Practice (Visualizing Vocabulary)

Help your student visualize important vocabulary by encouraging them to think of an image that is best associated with the word. To do this, it would be helpful to have your student look through images that are associated with the word. For example, when defining the term legislative branch, your student may think of bills or laws. Encourage your student to draw a bill or law to represent the key feature of the legislative branch, which is to create laws.

Practice (Bubble Map)

Assist your student in filling in the bubble map by selecting one branch of government to discuss together first. Model for your student how to return to the worktext to review the features of that branch. Help your student summarize these key features into a few phrases to write in the bubbles. Encourage your student to fill out the rest of the bubbles on their own, reminding them to return to the work text, and assisting them if needed in summarizing the key features of each into short phrases.

Practice (Forms of Democracy)

Help your student complete this table by asking them to review the worktext. Then ask your student to focus on one column at a time. For example, your student may state that a direct democracy features all people who come together to make decisions and laws in the second column. In the third column, your student may state that a direct democracy affects American life by giving people the freedom to make decisions, such as answering a referendum.

Learning Styles

Auditory learners may enjoy recording a song or a podcast to explain what democracy is, how it works, and its effects on American life. They may also enjoy giving a speech on a bill they believe should become a law.

Visual learners may enjoy drawing or digitally designing a persuasive advertisement for a bill that can help people and the environment, such as planting more trees, creating universal healthcare, lowering taxes, or protecting animals from being killed for their hides. A bill should focus on a specific topic.

Kinesthetic learners may enjoy creating a song that features the three branches of government or playing charades using vocabulary words.

Extension Activities

Vision Board
Inform your student that there are many ways to be an active participant in government and have a voice in society, such as volunteering in a soup kitchen, helping a classmate pick up plastic in the environment, or coming up with ideas to protect endangered animals. With your student, think about different ways you can help your community. Then encourage your student to visualize this process by creating a vision board that includes pictures and ideas. For example, if your student wants to protect endangered sea turtles, they can draw sea turtles or use an online search engine to find photos to add to their vision board. Your student may also list ideas that could help protect sea turtles, such as removing litter from the ocean.

Flow Chart
Help your student visualize the process of how a bill becomes a law by creating a flow chart. Encourage your student to start with where a bill starts, such as in the US House of Representatives. Then, ask your student to outline the additional steps that are needed. The flow chart should include the amount of members in the House and Senate that are needed to approve the bill, what happens when the bill goes to the president, and how a bill eventually becomes a law.

Answer Key

Write *(What kind of democracy does the United States have? Why did the Founding Fathers choose to use an electoral college rather than having the people vote themselves?)*
Answers will vary. Possible answer: The United States is an indirect democracy. This allows an easier way for a large amount of people to vote and voice their opinions.

Practice *(Visualizing Vocabulary)*
Check your student's definitions against the definitions provided in the previous lessons. Ask your student to explain how their drawings relate to each definition.

Practice *(Bubble Map)*
Answers will vary. Possible answers:

1. Features of the Executive Branch may include: signs and enforces laws; includes president, vice president, and the cabinet; president can nominate Supreme Court justices

2. Features of the Legislative Branch may include: creates new laws from bills; Congress is made up of the Senate and the House of Representatives; can declare war; can impeach president

3. Features of the Judicial Branch may include: decides if laws are legal; enforces constitution; includes Supreme Court and Supreme Court justices

Practice *(Forms of Democracy)*
Answers will vary. Possible answers:

Forms of Democracy	Features	How American Life Is Affected
Direct	All voters come together to make decisions and laws. Voting is done by using a referendum.	People have the freedom to speak and make decisions.
Indirect	People elect representatives to speak for them. People cannot create laws directly.	People have the right to have free and fair elections.

Quick Review

Refer to the statement your student circled in the Show What You Know section to self-assess their knowledge of the chapter concepts. Then to assist in determining if your student is ready to take the assessment, consider:

- Having your student review the bubble map they filled out in the Practice section. Look for the accuracy and quality of answers, such as key features of the executive, legislative, and judicial branches.
- Having your student describe in words or create a flow chart of how a bill becomes a law. Check for your student's understanding of the roles each branch of government has on the process of a bill becoming a law.
- Having your student describe the differences between direct and indirect democracy. Assess your student's understanding of the content by asking them to give examples from daily life of how democracy may have influenced them (i.e., the freedom to speak in class has given your student the opportunity to voice their opinions).

Discover! SOCIAL STUDIES • GRADE 4 • CHAPTER 4 ASSESSMENT

89

Chapter Assessment

Fill in the blanks using the vocabulary words in the word bank below.

Word Bank: bill   Congress   executive branch   referendum   legislative branch   judicial branch

1. Presidents, vice presidents, and the cabinet make up the _____.

2. The US House of Representatives and the US Senate are members of _____.

3. The _____ is responsible for creating laws.

4. Ideas are written on a _____ before it can become a law.

5. The _____ is responsible for deciding if laws are constitutional.

6. If I vote *yes* or *no* to making or changing a rule, I am voting by a _____.

Answer each of the questions below in complete sentences on the lines provided.

7. What is the Electoral College?

8. What are the two forms of democracy?

9. How does democracy influence American life?

10. How does a bill become a law?

Chapter Assessment Answer Key

1. executive branch
2. Congress
3. legislative branch
4. bill
5. judicial branch
6. referendum
7. Answers may vary. Possible answer: system of electors that were created to select the next president of the United States
8. direct democracy and indirect democracy
9. Answers may vary. Possible answers: by allowing people to participate in free and fair elections; by giving people the freedom to speak and make decisions
10. Answers may vary. Possible answers: First, ideas are written in a bill. Then, the bill gets reviewed and discussed in both the US House of Representatives and the US Senate. If two-thirds of representatives and two-thirds of senators pass the bill, the bill gets sent to the president. From there, the president can sign and pass the bill, which turns the bill into a law. Or the president can veto the bill. If the bill is vetoed, it can go back to the House or Senate for review and discussion. If two-thirds of representatives and two-thirds of senators still support the bill, the bill automatically becomes a law.

Alternative Assessment

Project: Infographic

Project Requirements or Steps:

You will create an infographic to show features of different government branches in the United States. An infographic is a chart or diagram used to convey information or data quickly and clearly. Use the following steps to create your infographic:

1. Select at least two government branches you studied in the chapter. Gather information about the features of these branches.

2. Create a title for your infographic related to the topic.

3. Include photos and drawings related to the topic.

4. Include information or data to explain and support the photos and drawings you included.

5. Include at least two similarities between the features of the government branches you selected.

6. Present the information in a creative way.

Alternative Assessment Rubric

Use the following rubric to grade your student's assessment.

	4	3	2	1	Points
Connection to the Chapter	The infographic is clearly connected to the chapter.	The infographic is connected to the chapter.	The infographic is somewhat connected to the chapter.	The infographic is not connected to the chapter.	
Creativity	The infographic is very creative and aesthetically appealing.	The infographic is creative and aesthetically appealing.	The infographic is somewhat creative and aesthetically appealing.	The infographic is not creative or aesthetically appealing.	
Information	The information or data is accurate and easy to follow.	The information or data is accurate.	The information or data is somewhat accurate.	The information or data is not accurate.	
Grammar and Mechanics	There are no grammar and punctuation mistakes.	There are one or two grammar and punctuation mistakes.	There are several grammar and punctuation mistakes.	There are a distracting number of grammar and punctuation mistakes.	

Total Points _____/16

Average _____

Discover! SOCIAL STUDIES • GRADE 4 • CHAPTER 4 ASSESSMENT

93

The Northwest Territory

Lesson Objectives

By the end of this lesson, your student will be able to:

- identify how the land in the Northwest Territory was organized and divided
- describe the rules that were established in the Northwest Ordinance and their effect on the Americans and the Indigenous people
- describe how the expansion into the Northwest Territory created conflict between Americans and Indigenous people and the effects of these conflicts

Supporting Your Student

Explore

Your student may struggle thinking about what it may have been like for the settlers that were traveling to a brand new area to start new lives. The questions that are asked should be discussed prior to starting the lesson. As you go through the lesson, refer back to these questions from time to time. This promotes empathy and true understanding of what the people during this time may have been going through.

Write *(Think about the rules in the Northwest Ordinance of 1787. Do you think everyone followed the rules? Do you think everyone agreed with these rules? Why or why not?)*

You can prompt your student to answer the question by providing examples of rules that we have in our society and at home. Ask your student if they agree or disagree with the societal and home rules. If they disagree with one or more, emphasize that this may be how the settlers were feeling too.

Practice

Your student may want to reread the information found under the heading "Conflict in The Northwest Territory." It would also be good for your student to think about one group—either the Indigenous people or the settlers—at a time. Start with the group they are feeling the most familiar with and then move onto the other group. Also, provide a list of words they could choose from to explain why they think the Indigenous people or the settlers were feeling that way.

Learning Styles

Auditory learners may enjoy reading parts of the lesson aloud to others or giving an oral report about one of the chiefs they learned about in the Online Connection activity.

Visual learners may enjoy drawing a map of the Northwest Territory or plotting out one of the townships from the Northwest Ordinance and thinking about how they would divide up the land.

Kinesthetic learners may enjoy plotting out one of the lots from the Northwest Ordinance by going outside to an open area and measuring it out. Each lot was 640 acres or 1 square mile each.

Extension Activities

Create a Journal

After completing the entire lesson, have your student write a journal entry as if they are one of the settlers in the Northwest Territory. They can use some of the questions that were asked of them in the Explore section. They can explain how their township is doing, what is going well, and what obstacles they have faced. They might describe what laws have been created in their township. They should draw any information they learned in the lesson.

Pros/Cons List

Have your student create a T-chart on a piece of paper. On the left side of the chart, write the title "Pros." On the right side of the chart, write the title "Cons." Have them make a list of all of the pros and cons that came out of the United States expansion into the Northwest Territory. They should use the ideas that they learned in the lesson. They can also make predictions as to what they think might happen as the United States continues to expand west into new territory.

Answer Key

Write *(Think about the rules in the Northwest Ordinance of 1787. Do you think everyone followed the rules? Do you think everyone agreed with these rules? Why or why not?)*
Answers may vary. Possible answers: Many people did not agree with the rules. Many people also did not follow the rules. This may have occurred because people did not think the rules were fair and did what they wanted to instead.

Practice
Answers may vary. Possible answers:

Thoughts/Feeling of the Indigenous People	Thoughts/Feelings of the Settlers
• unhappy about their land being taken away • difficulty communicating and understanding the settlers	• making a better life for their family • difficulty communicating and understanding the Indigenous people

Show What You Know
1. True

2. False

3. True

4. False

5. B, C

6. Answer may vary. Possible answer: Public education was to be provided, slavery was against the law, and people were free to practice their religion. We also cannot take land that belongs to someone else and each state has its own constitution.

7. Answer may vary. Possible answer: The settlers were taking land away from the Indigenous people, even after they agreed not to. This led to the two groups fighting. Additionally, the Indigenous people and the United States signed an agreement, but conflict still continued.

Lesson Objectives

By the end of this lesson, your student will be able to:

- identify the benefits of the Louisiana Territory purchase
- identify examples of natural resources the United States got access to when purchasing the Louisiana Territory
- trace a route down the Mississippi River on a map to show the path many people took to trade

Supporting Your Student

Explore

Your student may need to be prompted with some examples of deals you have made in order to start thinking about one of their own. Have your student brainstorm a list of deals they have made by asking them a guiding question, like "How did you solve the problem with _____ when you both wanted to play the game at the same time?" This is part of the activity in the sidebar as well, so this may help them to think about their own deals.

Write *(How did purchasing the Louisiana Territory from France benefit the United States?)*

Your student should be prompted to look back in the reading for answers. Once answers are found, have a discussion with your student about which benefit they believe was best for the United States. For example, discuss how the United States could now easily use the Mississippi River for trade. This would mean people and businesses could make more money.

Read *(Natural Resources in the Louisiana Territory)*

Have your student look at the images of the natural resources. Start by selecting one of the resources. Model for your student how this resource might have been beneficial to the settlers by saying how you use the resource. This might sound like "Today, we use fresh water to drink, and plants need water to grow. Settlers would've needed water to grow plants and crops too." Then have your student select another natural resource. This time, work together to think how this natural resource might have benefited the

settlers. If your student seems to be getting the hang of this, have them try to do this on their own. Connecting how these resources help us today with how the resources would've helped the settlers will help your student solidify this knowledge.

Practice

If your student struggles with drawing a picture, prompt them to look back at the previous page where there are pictures and captions of each natural resource. Walk your student through some of the resources and have them reread the captions. Ask them to tell you what the settlers used the resource for. Then, ask your student how they could draw that in a picture. You may also want to help your student with how they could create one scene and include multiple natural resources.

If your student struggles with writing about the natural resources, start by looking back at the pictures and captions on the previous page for ideas. They could also be offered sentence starters to help them. For example, "One of the natural resources the settlers in the Louisiana territory used was _____. They used this natural resource to help them _____."

Learning Styles

Auditory learners may enjoy listening to early American folk music that was popular with settlers during this time period.

Visual learners may enjoy drawing their own map of the United States and labeling the Louisiana Territory, the Mississippi River, and New Orleans. They may also enjoy including the Northwest Territory on their map from the previous lesson to compare and contrast the two territories.

Kinesthetic learners may enjoy exploring the area around their neighborhood to see how many natural resources they can identify. They can compare the resources they find to the resources that were found in the Louisiana Territory.

Extension Activities

Natural Resources Charades

Use strips of paper to write down the different ways the settlers in the Louisiana Territory used the natural resources in the area. For ideas, look in the Answer Key. Place all of the strips of paper in a bucket or hat. Have your student take turns picking one slip of paper and acting out what is on the slip. Friends or family members can guess what action they are doing and what natural resource they are using.

Move West Poster

Have your student create a poster or advertisement to convince people to move to the Louisiana Territory. Your student should include a map and write convincing points as to why someone would want to move and settle there. They should think about all of the positive things the territory had to offer, including its natural resources.

Answer Key

Explore

Answers may vary. Possible answers include:

- playing a group game and deciding who will be "it" or go first
- trading chores or jobs around the house for desserts or more tv time
- deciding with someone what to do first and then what to do after
- these deals can be made with friends, parents, and other grownups
- deals are fair if both sides are giving up something and getting something in return

Write (How did purchasing the Louisiana Territory from France benefit the United States?)

Answers may vary. Possible answers include: doubling the size of the land, helping the economy, providing a trade route using the Mississippi River and the port of New Orleans, gaining many helpful natural resources

Practice

Answers may vary. Possible answers:

- settlers using water to cook, drink, or send items down the river to trade
- settlers using trees or timber to build homes or other buildings in the territory
- settlers eating animals, making clothing from animals, or animals grazing on the land
- settlers planting crops or creating farmland
- settlers using minerals to treat wounds, paint a house or other building, or make sheets of copper for ships

Show What You Know

1. A, D, E
2. Answers may vary. Possible answers include:
   - water: drink, cook, trade
   - forests: building material
   - animals: eating, clothing
   - land: farming, building homes and towns
   - minerals: treating wounds, paint, hulls of ships
3. The Mississippi River should be colored blue.

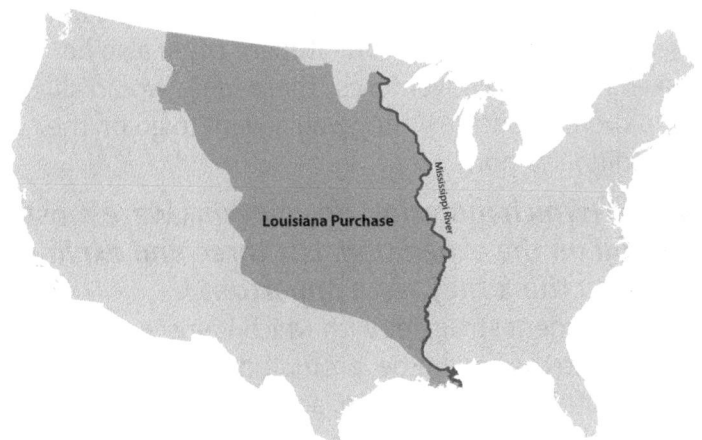

Lesson Objectives

By the end of this lesson, your student will be able to:

- identify the importance of the Lewis and Clark Expedition
- explain the role Sacagawea played in creating relationships with Indigenous people during the Lewis and Clark Expedition
- analyze a primary source, such as a map of the Lewis and Clark Expedition
- list appropriate materials, including tools and food, that would be needed for a long expedition

Supporting Your Student

Explore

If your student struggles with deciding whether or not they would go on the expedition, they might be prompted to look at the map and think about the distance of the journey. They should also be reminded that the land had never been explored by settlers before. Ask your student, "What did the settlers encounter when they explored the Northwest Territory?" Your student should be reminded of the settlers' encounters with the Indigenous people and how there was conflict. Your student could also be asked if they like adventures. These ideas would all help them to decide if they would want to go on the expedition or not.

Write *(Which materials do you think were most helpful on the expedition. List three and explain why you think they were important.)*

If your student struggles with which items were most important, they might be prompted to go back to the list of the supplies. Then, ask your student which three items would they most want to have with them if they were going on a long trip. You may also want to guide your student to only pick one thing from each of the bulleted lists to help to make sure they have at least one item from different categories.

Practice

Ask your student how Sacagawea helped Lewis and Clark. What was she able to do that they could not? (Translate, let the other Indigenous people know they were friendly) As your student looks at the map, help them to think about the benefits of splitting up on the expedition. What could Lewis and Clark do to learn about more land areas? What could Lewis and Clark do to maybe find a water route all the way to the Pacific Ocean?

Show What You Know

Your student could make flashcards on items Lewis and Clark brought on their journey and things they did not prior to completing the Show What You Know. They can practice sorting these items into piles of things they brought and things they did not bring. Your student could make a Venn diagram of pros and cons of the expedition. This will help them think about the importance of the expedition. Pros: new map, animals, and plants found, made friends with the Indigenous people. Cons: They were gone for a long time, they did not find a water route to the Pacific Ocean.

Learning Styles

Auditory learners may enjoy searching the language of the Shoshone people (the language Sacagawea helped to translate) and learning how to say a few words in that language.

Visual learners may enjoy creating a detailed map or a timeline of the Lewis and Clark expedition from start to finish.

Kinesthetic learners may enjoy learning to use a compass to get from one place to another, just as Lewis and Clark did on their expedition.

Extension Activities

Write a Letter

Have your student pretend that they are President Thomas Jefferson. Have them write a letter to Meriwether Lewis asking him to lead the expedition. They should try to persuade Lewis to go. Your student should also explain what he would like them to see accomplished while on the expedition.

Cooking

Recreate a meal that Lewis and Clark made and ate while on their expedition. Simple recipes can be found in books from the library or by using a search engine on the computer.

Answer Key

Explore

Answers may vary. Possible answers:

- Yes, I would go on the expedition because I love exploring. I would be a little nervous, but I would also be excited about discovering new things.

- No, I would not go. That journey sounds way too scary. I would be scared that I would fight with the Indigenous people. I would not want to be gone from my family for that long.

Write *(Which materials do you think were most helpful on the expedition? List three and explain why you think they were important.)*

Answers may vary. Possible answers:

- Food: to survive in case they are not able to hunt right away
- Fishing equipment: to catch fish to eat
- Guns or knives: for protection and for getting food
- Gifts for the Indigenous people: so they would be friendly and Lewis and Clark could continue their expedition
- Compass: so they could go in the right direction and not get lost
- Journal: to draw maps to bring back to President Jefferson

Practice

1. Answers may vary. Possible answers: being an interpreter, being a guide, helping to let the other Indigenious people know the expedition was friendly, or getting horses to cross the mountains

2. Answers may vary. Possible answers: It helped them to explore more of the area and learn more information to bring back. They were able to create more maps and maybe find more plants and animals to bring back.

Show What You Know

1. A, B, C
2. A, D, E, F
3. A, B, D
4. Answers may vary. Possible answers: being an interpreter, being a guide, helping to let the other Indigenious people know the expedition was friendly, or getting horses to cross the mountains

Lesson Objectives

By the end of this lesson, your student will review the following big ideas from Chapter 5.

- The settlers and the Indigenous people had many conflicts during the expansion into the Northwest Territory. (Lesson 33)
- The United States expanded into the Louisiana Territory. This new territory offered new trade routes and supplied the United States with many valuable natural resources. (Lesson 34)
- President Thomas Jefferson asked Lewis and Clark to lead an expedition of men across the Louisiana Territory all the way to the Pacific Ocean to explore the new territory. (Lesson 35)
- The Lewis and Clark Expedition was very successful. They created new maps of the land and brought back new plant and animal life. (Lesson 35)
- During the Lewis and Clark Expedition, the Indigenous people were key to the success of the journey. Sacagawea, a Shoshone woman, guided and translated for Lewis and Clark during most of the expedition. (Lesson 35)

Supporting Your Student

Review (The Northwest Territory and The Louisiana Territory)

As you read with your student, be sure to point out similarities between the two territories. For example, they both expanded the United States to the west. Additionally, be sure to point out differences between the two. For example, the Northwest Territory was obtained after the French and Indian War in 1763. The Louisiana Territory was obtained in 1803 through a purchase from France. This will help your student better understand the sequence of events and that these two territories were acquired at separate times.

Write (What was one effect of people settling westward had on the Indigenous people?)

With your student, reread the section "Settlers and the Indigenous People." There are many effects in that section. For example, the conflict caused the

Northwest Indian War. Additionally, after the war, it caused the Indigenous people to have to relocate.

Practice (Visualizing Vocabulary)

Prompt your student to go back and look through the definitions of the vocabulary words again. Have your student talk through the definitions and explain in their own words what they mean. Your student may also have an easier time putting words together that come from the same lesson. They may also find making flash cards helpful in studying vocabulary words.

Practice (Sequencing the Events of the Explorations West)

Your student should start by deciding if each statement is referring to the Northwest Territory, the Louisiana Territory, or the Lewis and Clark Expedition. Then they should be reminded of the order of the lessons: Northwest Territory first, Louisiana Territory second, and Lewis and Clark third. This will help them put the statements in order if they first divide them into categories by lesson.

Learning Styles

Auditory learners may enjoy creating a documentary about the chapter to share with their friends. They may also enjoy creating a podcast about the cause and effects of the United States expanding west.

Visual learners may enjoy creating a mural on a large piece of paper of the most important points from each lesson. They may also enjoy visuals of the vocabulary words. They might also enjoy a graphic organizer of the big ideas from the chapter: expansion to the west (Northwest Territory and Louisiana Purchase), the Lewis and Clark Expedition, and the effects on the Indigenous people.

Kinesthetic learners may enjoy acting out the cause and effects of different events. For example, they can act out being Thomas Jefferson explaining to Lewis and Clark why they should explore the West. They may also enjoy exploring the Lewis and Clark trail virtually, or if they live nearby, they could go to one of the spots they explored.

Extension Activities

Writing Questions

Have your student look back at each of the lesson objectives from the three lessons in the chapter. Have your student come up with a question they could ask another student about that objective. They should also come up with the answer to that question. Your student could make true or false, multiple choice, or short response questions.

Create a Tri-Fold Brochure

Have your student create a brochure with key points from each lesson in the chapter. The front of the brochure should have the chapter name and title. Each of the three parts inside should have the key information from each of the three lessons: the Northwest Territory, the Louisiana Purchase, and the Lewis and Clark Expedition.

Answer Key

Write *(What was one effect of people settling westward had on the Indigenous people?)*
This created conflict leading to the Northwest Indian War, which the United States won. Many of the Indigenous people were relocated to different areas.

Write *(Why was Sacagawea important to the success of the Lewis and Clark Expedition?)*
She was able to translate for them and was familiar with the difficult terrain.

Practice *(Visualizing Vocabulary)*
Answers will vary. Possible Answers: Make sure that whichever words your student picks are depicted in the picture and that both words are used in the sentence below the picture. Possible answers:

• We used the port to ship the natural resources.
• We found many useful natural resources in the new territory.
• We had to create ordinances for the new territory.
• The ordinances help reduce conflict.
• I have a conflict with an alliance that has different views than I do.
• There was no conflict on the expedition because everyone got along.

Practice *(Sequencing the Events of the Explorations West)*
Your student should place the events in the following order:

1. B
2. E
3. D
4. A
5. F
6. C

Practice *(Cause and Effect)*

Cause	Effect
The United States gained new territory to the west after the French and Indian War and the Louisiana Purchase.	The desire to explore the West. Thomas Jefferson enlisted Lewis and Clark to lead an expedition.
After the Land Ordinance of 1785, new people settled west where Indigenous people were already living.	The Northwest Indian War conflict happened.
The United States won the Northwest Indian War and gained control of the land.	Indigenous people were relocated from their native lands.

Quick Review

Refer to the statement your student circled in the Show What You Know section to self-assess their knowledge of the chapter concepts. Then to assist in determining if your student is ready to take the assessment, consider:

- Having your student create a poster with drawings and text to explain how the expansion west benefited the United States.

- Having your student look at a map and identify the area that was the Northwest Territory, the area that was the Louisiana Territory, the Mississippi River, and the route Lewis and Clark took on their expedition.

- Having your student create a song about what the relationships were like between the settlers/explorers and the Indigenous people in each of the lessons.

Chapter Assessment

Circle all the correct answers.

1. What were Thomas Jefferson's goals for the Lewis and Clark expedition?

   A. learn about the landforms, plants, and animals of the region

   B. meet the Indigenous people who lived in the region and learn more about them

   C. build roads for travel west

   D. find a water route to the Pacific Ocean

2. What rules were set up in the Northwest Territory that we still use today?

   A. public education must be provided

   B. slavery was not allowed

   C. public health care must be provided

   D. people could practice their own religion

3. Why was Sacagawea important to the success of the Lewis and Clark Expedition?

   A. she could interpret for them

   B. she was able to guide them through the difficult terrain

   C. she was an expert rock climber

   D. she was the leader of the expedition

4. What was one benefit of the Louisiana Purchase for the United States?

   A. they were able to be friends with the Indigenous people

   B. they were able to double the size of the United States

   C. they had more access to natural resources

   D. they had control of all of North America

5. Why was there conflict between the Indigenous people and the settlers that came to the Northwest Territory?

   ....

   ....

   ....

   ....

Discover! SOCIAL STUDIES • GRADE 4 • CHAPTER 5 ASSESSMENT

103

6. What is one similarity and one difference between the Northwest Territory and the Louisiana Territory?

....

....

....

....

Chapter Assessment Answer Key

1. A, B, D
2. A, B, D
3. A, B
4. B, C
5. They were not able to communicate with each other. The settlers were taking over land that belonged to the Indigenous people. The Indigenous people did not feel this was fair.
6. Answers will vary. Possible answers: Both territories expanded the United States to the west. The Louisiana Territory was purchased from France and the Northwest Territory was obtained through a treaty after the French and Indian War.

Discover! SOCIAL STUDIES • GRADE 4 • CHAPTER 5 ASSESSMENT

105

Alternative Assessment

Project: Diary

Project Requirements or Steps:

Complete a diary entry or a series of diary entries about your own observations or fictional observations based on the unit. You will pretend to be on the Lewis and Clark Expedition. Write about observations you would make on the journey and how you might feel.

1. Date
2. Important events that occurred or relate to the unit
3. Emotional response and thoughts to events or the unit
4. Examples that connect the topic to the unit or lesson
5. Definitions of key terms

106

Discover! SOCIAL STUDIES • GRADE 4 • CHAPTER 5 ASSESSMENT

Alternative Assessment Rubric

Use the following rubric to grade your student's assessment.

	4	3	2	1	Points
Connection to the Chapter	The diary makes clear and repetitive connections to the chapter.	The diary is connected to the chapter.	The diary is somewhat connected to the chapter.	The diary is not connected to the chapter.	
Creativity and Neatness	The diary is presented very neatly, and the topic shows creativity and originality.	The diary is presented very neatly, and the topic is somewhat original and creative.	The diary is basic and somewhat neat.	The diary is not neat or creative.	
Quality of Content	The content of the diary is personal and reveals the author's thoughts and feelings. It is very detailed and interesting.	The content of the diary is somewhat personal and talks briefly about the author's thoughts and feelings. It has a few details and is somewhat interesting.	The content of the diary is not very personal and has only one or two comments about the author's thoughts and feelings. It is not very interesting.	The diary is not personal or interesting.	
Grammar and Mechanics	There are no grammar and punctuation mistakes.	There are one or two grammar and punctuation mistakes.	There are several grammar and punctuation mistakes.	There are a distracting number of grammar and punctuation mistakes.	

Total Points _____/16

Average _____

Discover! SOCIAL STUDIES • GRADE 4 • CHAPTER 5 ASSESSMENT

107

Lesson Objectives

By the end of this lesson, your student will be able to:

- identify the reasons for the War of 1812
- analyze the reasons that the United States and Great Britain were not prepared to enter into another war
- identify the similarities and differences of the navies from the United States and Great Britain during the War of 1812

Supporting Your Student

Create

To help your student create a treaty, first discuss possible conflicts in your student's life that might necessitate a treaty. Do they argue about their bedtime, screen time, or wake-up time? Perhaps they disagree with a sibling regarding a particular toy or game. In choosing a real conflict your student experiences, this activity will become meaningful and engaging. Discuss the word *compromise*. Each party should feel the treaty is fair. This means most likely neither person will get everything they want. Your student should meet with the individual with whom they have the conflict and take notes regarding their compromise or agreed-on solution. The treaty should explain what each participant will do or how their actions will change. Your student can number these changes, use bullet points in a list, or write in essay form. Then both subjects of the treaty should sign it.

Explore

As your student reads this section, encourage them to highlight or underline unfamiliar words such as vessel and navy. Tell them that these words will be very important in the coming sections of the text. Use the glossary or look up these words online to build their background knowledge. After your student reads this section, have them close their eyes and practice visualizing. Reread the text to them while they use their imagination to visualize what takes place in the text.

Read (*Conflicts at Home and Sea*)

With events involving several countries and taking place on the Atlantic Ocean and northern United States, keeping a world map handy or a map of the United States from 1812 is recommended during this lesson. Encourage your student to find Great Britain, the Atlantic Ocean, Canada, and the eastern coast of the United States on a map. Finding the Louisiana Purchase territory may also help them understand that the United States looked very different during this period.

Learning Styles

Auditory learners may enjoy a word of the day challenge. Challenge your student to use a tricky vocabulary word when speaking. When they use this word they can give themselves a point on a tally chart and vice versa.

Visual learners may enjoy referring to maps when new locations are introduced. Print out a world map and encourage your student to label important places from the chapter.

Kinesthetic learners may enjoy crafting their own merchant vessel or navy frigate out of materials they find at home. They may also enjoy acting out a trade by exchanging small items with a sibling or friend.

Extension Activities

US Map in 1812

Print a blank copy of North America, or have your student draw their own outline. Support your student in locating maps from 1812 online to print or copy. Have your student outline the US states in red. Then outline US territory, areas that were not yet a state, in green. Frontier lands should be outlined in yellow. Territories or colonies of other countries should be outlined in purple. Your student can create a key to show the meaning of each color.

Native American Experience: Tecumseh Biography

Tecumseh is an important figure in the War of 1812. Your student may be curious to know more about this man's life. This curiosity can be encouraged in a biography project. Begin by telling your student that biographies share information about the life of a real person. In order to learn more about Tecumseh, visit websites online and read about his life. Encourage your student to fold a piece of paper into three sections and to write notes from the beginning of Tecumseh's life in the first section, the middle of his life in the second section, and the end of his life in the third section.

Your student should reread their notes and number the facts they wish to include in their writing. They can cross out or change the numbering as they go. This can help them write facts in order when they begin writing their biography.

Have your student write at least three paragraphs about Tecumseh's life. If you wish to take this project further, work on including introductory and conclusion paragraphs as well as a rough and final draft.

Answer Key

Explore

Answers will vary. Possible answers: Maybe the British navy wants to steal the ship or take prisoners. I would feel scared and angry after this experience. I would expect my government to rescue the men who were taken.

Write (What reasons did the United States have for getting involved in another war with Great Britain?)

Ansewrs may vary. Possible answers: Impressment and restrictions on trade were reasons for getting involved in a war with Great Britain. British support of Native American resistance to westward expansion was also a reason for war.

Write (Would you rather be a member of the British Royal Navy or the United States Navy in the 1800s?)

Answers will vary. Possible answers: I would rather be a member of the British navy because their navy was larger and stronger. I would rather be a member of the American navy because their ships were faster and the British were already at war with France.

Write (Why was the United States hesitant about declaring war with Great Britain? Who did the United States seem to be underestimating?)

Answers may vary. Possible answers: The United States was concerned that Great Britain's navy was too large and strong for America to succeed in another war. Many Americans did not want to get involved in a war because the US army was small and weak. Also, the eastern states wanted to focus on building the shipping industry and trade with other nations. The United States seemed to be underestimating the British colonies in Canada and their relationship with Native American warriors.

Practice

Pros	Cons
America wanted Great Britain to stop the impressment of US citizens.	The US military was not as strong as Great Britain's.
The United States wanted to be able to trade freely with other countries.	Eastern states wanted to focus on trade.
Great Britain was influencing Native Americans, causing more conflicts.	The Revolutionary War had recently ended, and many citizens did not want to enter another war so soon.

Show What you Know

1. A

2. B

3. False

4. Answers may vary. Possible answer: They were forcing American citizens to fight for their navy. This was called impressment.

Online Connection

Answers will vary. Possible answers: The maps are different because there were only 19 states in the United States at the time of the War of 1812. There were large territories not yet states as well as land part of the frontier, which had not been settled by the United States. The United States was trying to occupy and settle all lands between the Atlantic and Pacific oceans.

Lesson Objectives

By the end of this lesson, your student will be able to:

- identify why the Battle of New Orleans occurred despite a treaty being in place between the United States and Great Britain
- evaluate how the War of 1812 affected America
- describe American military engagements in Canada that did not succeed
- explain how Americans showed patriotism, including Francis Scott Key and Dolley Madison

Supporting Your Student

Explore

Analyzing "The Star-Spangled Banner" may require providing some extra support for your student as several vocabulary words may be unfamiliar. The poet is describing the scene following an important battle, the Battle of Fort McHenry. The soldiers raised a large flag that could be seen over the ramparts, or battlements, which were parts of a fort that soldiers could shoot through while keeping cover. The glare, or light, from the cannons allowed everyone to see the flag. This showed everyone that the fort had not been captured.

Read *(Expectations of Victory)*

Draw your student's attention to the map of the Great Lakes region to help illustrate where fighting began in the War of 1812. Find the city of Detroit, Lake Erie, the Niagara River, and Lake Ontario. Looking at the map, ask your student why this region's capture could be beneficial to the United States. You can prompt your student by recalling that transportation at the time was limited to ships, horses, carriages, and by foot. The rivers and lakes in this area would be valuable assets for both countries as they allowed for the transportation of people and supplies by ship.

Take a Closer Look *(A Hero to the People)*

Your student may have further questions regarding Andrew Jackson's heroism. Analyzing his role in the War of 1812 and his presidency can provide an opportunity to discuss changing perspectives over time. An individual hailed as a hero by one generation may not be seen as such by a future generation. Ongoing debates in society exist over such issues, and you can encourage your student to develop their own opinion and support it with facts they learn through study.

Learning Styles

Auditory learners may enjoy listening to an audio version of "The Star Spangled Banner." They might also enjoy using repetition and rhyme throughout the reading. They can even practice writing a line of silly poetry. Encourage students to repeat the names of battles and think of a rhyming word. For example, McHenry rhymes with envy. The British were filled with envy after Fort McHenry!

Visual learners may enjoy taking notes on two colors of sticky pads or two colors of paper. The first color is dedicated to American victories, and the second to British victories. Finding videos about "The Star Spangled Banner" or the War of 1812 can help bring the content to life as well.

Kinesthetic learners may enjoy creating a special salute for American soldiers and a different salute for British soldiers. Encourage your student to use the salute when reading about a particular navy or army in battle. Your student can create a fort out of craft supplies or a map illustrating important battles from the War of 1812.

Extension Activities

Verse Writing

Tell your student that poems can be turned into songs. Listen to "The Star Spangled Banner" and remind your student that the song began as a poem. Ask your student to write their own patriotic verse for the song or create their own patriotic song or poem. Have your student perform their song or poem for family or friends.

Great Lakes Labeling

Have your student draw a map of the Great Lakes Region. Ask them to label the locations of battles discussed in the worktext on their map and to research other battles to include on their map. Have your student place a blue dot next to the battles won by the American troops and a red dot next to the battles won by the British troops. Then have your student make a color key for their map.

Answer Key

Explore

Answers will vary. Possible answers: The words *gallantly* and *perilous* show how brave he feels America has been. No, I am not surprised. He must have witnessed American soldiers' bravery during the battle.

Write (How did battles with British colonists in Canada surprise the US forces?)

Answers will vary. Possible answers: America thought territory in Canada would be easily conquered.

Write (Do you feel the Treaty of Ghent was fair? What would you add to the treaty?)

Answers will vary. Possible answers: I felt the treaty should have included an agreement to stop all impressment. I would add this provision if I was writing the treaty.

Practice

Answers will vary. Possible answers: The Native Americans helped strengthen the Canadian forces. The British were able to win battles and prevent the United States from taking Canadian territory.

Answers will vary. Possible answers: There was greater unity amongst the citizens of the country. The Native Americans' tribal alliance had ended. Westward expansion would continue unhindered.

Patriot	Proof of Patriotism
Dolley Madison	The first lady rescued a portrait of George Washington.
Francis Scott Key	He wrote the national anthem.
Andrew Jackson	He protected the city of New Orleans.

Show What You Know

1. B, C, D
2. B
3. Answers will vary. Possible answer: They became patriotic heroes.
4. False

Take a Closer Look (Weapons of the War of 1812)

Answers will vary. Possible answers: I think their supplies and weapons must have made fighting and traveling very difficult. It would be hard to move quickly from battle to battle.

Monroe Doctrine and Missouri Compromise

Lesson Objectives

By the end of this lesson, your student will be able to:

- summarize the viewpoints of opposing sides of the debate that resulted in the Missouri Compromise
- describe the main principles of the Monroe Doctrine

Supporting Your Student

Explore

After reading the explore section, explain to your student that the issue of slavery was about actual people. People who were experiencing slavery were mistreated. It is crucial your student understands slavery involved real people and was a real issue in the United States. Understanding how both sides felt will help them answer why the United States was divided over the Missouri Compromise. The South felt states should hold power to decide, and the North did not want any extension of the institution of slavery.

Read (The Missouri Compromise)

Before reading, it would be beneficial to review the Louisiana Territory in Chapter 34. The Missouri Compromise addressed whether new areas in the Louisiana Territory could be slave states or free states when they applied for statehood.

Read (The Monroe Doctrine)

After reading, it would be helpful to review the principles of the Monroe Doctrine listed in the sidebar. To check for understanding, have your student summarize the four points in their own words.

Practice

Terms to look for about the Missouri Compromise are *free state* and *slave state*, *balance*, and *North and South views*. Look for *Western Hemisphere affairs*, *European affairs*, and *colonization* as keywords to the Monroe Doctrine. Highlighting these phrases and words will help your student effectively sort the facts to the correct spot.

Learning Styles

Auditory learners may enjoy recording their voice summarizing the main concepts of the Monroe Doctrine to listen to as a review.

Visual learners may enjoy graphic organizers, organizing the different viewpoints of both sides of the Missouri Compromise.

Kinesthetic learners may enjoy highlighting the four main points of the Monroe Doctrine in the sidebar *The Four Main Purposes of the Monroe Doctrine*.

Extension Activities

Debate

Have a debate about the Missouri Compromise. Have your student choose a side: North or South. You, the instructor, take the opposing side. For the South, be sure to focus on states' rights, not whether slavery should be allowed or not. The South's main argument against the Missouri Compromise was that states should have the power to decide the laws, like whether slavery would be allowed.

Brochure

Have your student design a brochure explaining the main components of the Monroe Doctrine. The brochure should include an explanation of what the Monroe Doctrine was and the four primary principles. The student should also have illustrations in the brochure.

Answer Key

Explore
The United States was divided because the South wanted states to decide whether slavery should be allowed. The North did not want slavery to expand in the new territory and wanted to keep the balance between free and slave states.

Write *(What was the view of slave states on the Missouri Compromise?)*
They felt a state should decide whether it would be a free state or slave state.

Practice *(Sort the Facts)*

Monroe Doctrine	Missouri Compromise
• Closed colonization of the Americas to Europe • Declared Europe cannot interfere with affairs in the Americas • Declared if Europe interfered with any countries of the Americas, the United States would view it as a hostile action • The United States would recognize colonies of Europe already established in the Americas	• Maine entered the United States as a free state • A way to keep the balance between free states and slave states • Did not address the question of whether slavery would continue in the United States

Show What You Know

1. B
2. B
3. C
4. True
5. False
6. There are four main points of the Monroe Doctrine. European countries would not interfere with America's affairs or continue to colonize. The United States would recognize existing European colonies in the Americas. The United States would not interfere with European affairs, and any interference from Europe would be viewed as hostile.
7. Southern states disagreed with the Missouri Compromise because they felt states should decide whether they would be free or slave states.
8. Northern states disagreed because they did not want the extension of slavery in the new territory.

Lesson Objectives

By the end of this lesson, your student will be able to:

- explain how communities benefited from developments in canals, steamboats, roads, and the postal system
- describe how the railroad was important to the growth and development of the United States
- describe how factories developed across New England

Supporting Your Student

Read (Developments and Benefits of Canals, Steamboats, and Roads)

Before reading, create a graphic organizer labeled "Benefits of Transportation." Next, create three sections: canals, steamboats, and roads. When your student is reading, have them find one to two benefits to write under the type of transport. This will help your student organize the information and can be referenced later.

Read (New England Factories)

After reading, it would be helpful to show pictures of watermills and a map of New England so your student can see the many rivers. An extension would be locating cities and seeing where they are in relation to the rivers. Many towns in New England are located near rivers because factories needed the rivers for the watermills.

Read (Effects of Industrialization)

It would be helpful for your student to create two lists. One list is the benefits of industrialization, and the other is the disadvantages. Doing this will help organize the information and make it easy to reference later.

Practice

Have your student create a flowchart of how different modes of transport led to industrialization, the postal service being more effective, and the connection between the West and East Coast. Then have your student summarize their chart. They can draw out the cause and effect or write about it. This gives multiple ways to show their understanding of the text.

Learning Styles

Auditory learners may enjoy creating a podcast explaining how the railroads affected the United States.

Visual learners may enjoy creating graphic organizers showing the cause and effect. For example, the development of steamboats caused travel times to be faster, making transport more effective.

Kinesthetic learners may enjoy a field trip to a local canal or railroad tracks. This will help connect the learning to their life in a hands-on way.

Extension Activities

Pros and Cons

Have your student create a list of the pros and cons of railroad construction. For example, a pro is a transcontinental railroad connecting the two coasts of the United States. A con is it cuts through Indigenous land. Have your student use the worktext and online research to complete the list. Tell them to try to have five pros and five cons.

Research a New England Factory

Have your student research factories in the 19th century that were located in New England. Have them choose one and create a poster explaining what the factory made, what it was called, its years of operation, and two additional facts they wish to include. Some companies that owned factories to start their research are; Boston Associates' mills, Lawrence Manufacturing Company, and Lowell Factories.

Answer Key

Explore *(Why is it important that communities in the United States are connected?)*

Answers will vary. Possible answers: It was important to be connected to move materials. It was important to be connected so people could talk to loved ones and get important information.

(What design helped connect the United States?)

The railroad helped connect the US communities.

Write *(What was one benefit of steamboats?)*

One benefit was it cut travel times in half.

Write *(Name two effects of the railroad.)*

Answers will vary. Possible answers:

1. Able to transport materials from the West to factories in the East

2. More effective mail delivery

Practice *(Cause and Effect)*

Answers and drawings will vary possible answers: Your student should include how transportation affected the development of factories and the postal service.

Show What You Know

1. B
2. C
3. A
4. True
5. False
6. False
7. True
8. A, C, D
9. D
10. A, B, C, D

Sidebar *(Create)*

Maps will vary but should include a map key and a canal.

Lesson Objectives

By the end of this lesson, your student will review the following big ideas from Chapter 6.

- Great Britain's Navy was the largest and most powerful in the world. The US Navy was small, but its ships were strong and fast. (Lesson 37)
- The War of 1812 increased American patriotism and continued westward expansion. (Lesson 38)
- The Missouri Compromise tried and failed to address the issue of slavery. The Monroe Doctrine was an important document for US foreign policy. (Lesson 39)
- The development of roads, the railroad, canals, and steamboats impacted industrial development. (Lesson 40)

Supporting Your Student

Review *(Missouri Compromise, Monroe Doctrine, and Transportation)*

You may want to talk to your student about the issues with slavery regarding the Missouri Compromise. You may need to discuss how some states wanted to be slave states and other states did not want slave states.

Write *(How did transportation improve the postal system?)*

Transportation improved the postal system in many ways. Have your student first list the three or four types of transportation that were created. Have your student discuss the ways that these modes of transportation helped the postal system deliver mail and packages.

Practice *(Cause and Effect)*

If your student is struggling with completing this graphic organizer, you may want to ask questions to your student for each event. "What happened after England needed sailors?" and "What did England do?" For the second event, you may want to ask, "Why did the United States want England to stop colonizing areas like Lake Erie?" Continue to ask questions like these for the other events, if needed.

Learning Styles

Auditory learners may enjoy watching or listening to a video about the War of 1812. Your student may want to discuss new information that they learned about the War of 1812 with their instructor.

Visual learners may enjoy looking at images of transportation mentioned in the text including images of steamboats, railroads, and roads. Have your student look at a graph or chart showing how fast these modes of transportation can travel across the country or for a certain period of time.

Kinesthetic learners may enjoy creating a comic strip showing the events of the War of 1812. They should first list the events in the order in which they happened, and then write a sentence for each event in a box of a comic strip. Have your student draw and color the pictures.

Extension Activities

War of 1812 Map

Have your student research online the major battles and events of the War of 1812. Also, have them research an important fact for each battle or event. On a blank map, ask them to label each battle and event and draw pictures that depict the fact about each battle and event.

Monroe Doctrine Skit

Create a skit about the Monroe Doctrine. Your student may want to write the skit including what the European nations and the United States government might discuss if they got together to discuss the Monroe Doctrine. You can have your student and others act it out.

Answer Key

Write *(Describe the turning point in the War of 1812. What happened to the United States during the turning point?)*

The turning point of the War of 1812 was when the United States took control of Lake Erie and started winning the battles.

Write *(How did transportation improve the postal system?)*

When steamboats and canals were invented, then the postal system could send letters down river. When the transcontinental railroad was created, the mail and packages could be sent across the country quickly.

Practice *(One Word Doesn't Belong)*

1. territories; Impressment is when sailors were forced to join the British Navy.

2. steamboat; The national anthem and Dolley Madison's actions during the War of 1812 showed patriotism.

3. manufacturing; The Missouri Compromise has to do with slavery because it determined which states would be slave states and free states.

4. capture; The Monroe Doctrine wanted to stop European nations from colonization in America.

5. British Navy; Transportation grew with the Cumberland Road, Erie Canal, and transcontinental railroad.

Practice *(Cause and Effect)*

Cause	Effect
England needed sailors and wanted to punish the United States for trading with France.	Impressment happened by England forcing American sailors to fight for the British Navy.
The United States wanted expansion.	The War of 1812 began due to England's colonization of Lake Erie.
The United States only had 16 ships.	The United States realized they were not prepared for the war when they lost the first few battles.
British troops set the US Capitol on fire.	Dolley Madison ran inside and saved important documents and a portrait of Washington.
People did not know the war had ended, and the treaty was not ratified yet.	The Battle of New Orleans took place after the Treaty of Ghent was signed to end the war.

Practice *(Expansion and Transportation Growth)*

Answers will vary. Possible answer: The United States wanted to expand their land from coast to coast. Therefore, they wanted the European nations to stop colonizing areas within America. So they created the Monroe Doctrine, which caused European nations to stop colonization in America. The United States would then stop interfering with their government. Due to acquiring so much land, a transcontinental railroad was built, so now it would go from one coast to the other. A national road called the Cumberland Road was built for easier transportation, as well as steamboats and canals.

Quick Review

Refer to the statement your student circled in the Show What You Know section to self-assess their knowledge of the chapter concepts. Then to assist in determining if your student is ready to take the assessment, consider:

- Having your student describe the causes of the War of 1812, including expansion and colonization.
- Having your student describe the effects of the War of 1812, including England winning the first few battles, and then the United States winning Lake Erie and battles near the end of the war.
- Having your student name which states would be slave states and free states under the Missouri Compromise.
- Having your student explain how the Monroe Doctrine stopped colonization in the United States by European nations.
- Having your student describe the impact of transportation that advanced with the transcontinental railroad, national roads, canals, and the invention of the steamboa.

Discover! SOCIAL STUDIES • GRADE 4 • CHAPTER 6 ASSESSMENT

119

Chapter Assessment

Circle the correct answer.

1. Which of the following is a reason for the War of 1812?

    A. interfering in foreign policies

    B. US expansion

    C. need for better transportation

    D. creation of the postal service

2. What event determined which states entering the Union would be a free state or a slave state?

    A. Monroe Doctrine

    B. Lake Erie

    C. War of 1812

    D. Missouri Compromise

3. How did communities benefit from canals and steamboats?

    A. People could take vacations more.

    B. People could send goods and travel more quickly.

    C. People could watch the steamboats in the canals.

    D. It gave communities more jobs.

4. Where is the Erie Canal located on the map?

    A. Location A

    B. Location B

    C. Location C

    D. Location D

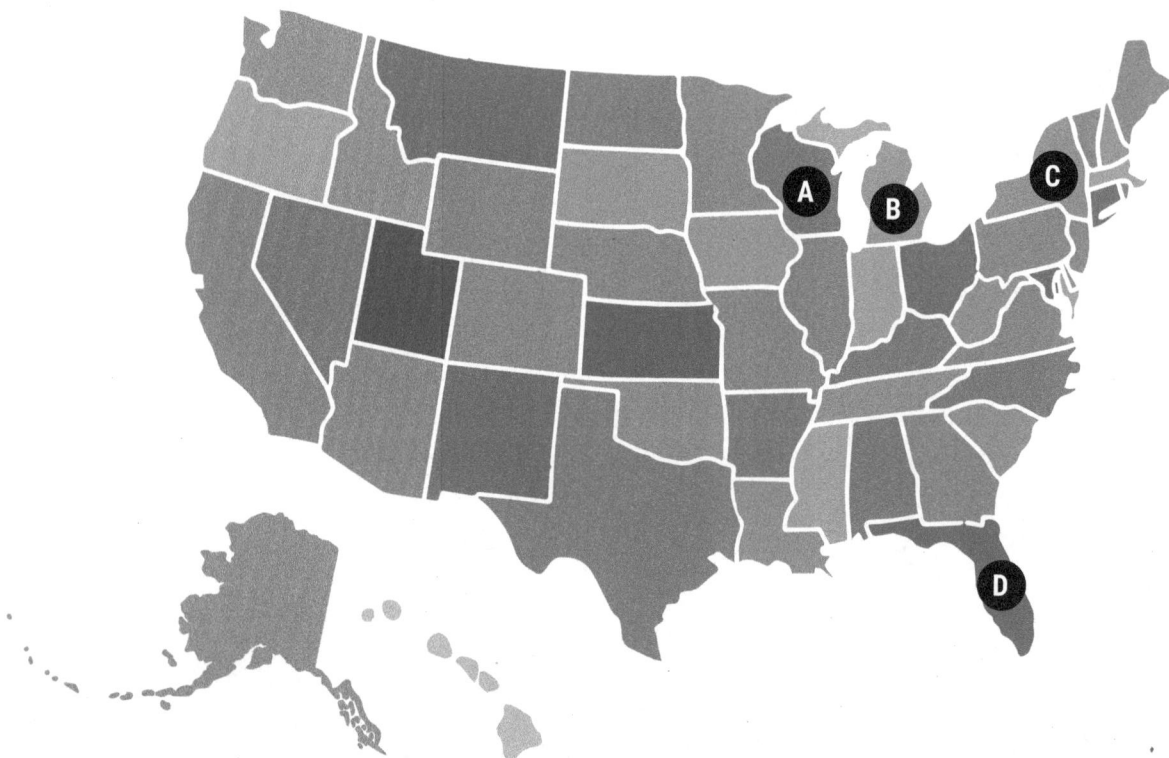

5. True or False   The Battle of New Orleans occurred after the Treaty of Ghent was signed to end the War of 1812.

6. True or False   The War of 1812 affected America because it killed many Americans.

7. True or False   General Block wrote the national anthem, "The Star-Spangled Banner."

8. True or False   The Missouri Compromise stopped the colonization in America by the European nations.

9. True or False   Factories developed across New England because there were more rivers.

Fill in the blank with the correct words.

10. The United States only had _____ ships and England had _____ ships when the War of 1812 started.

11. England was not prepared to fight in the War of 1812 because it was already fighting a war with _____.

12. _____ saved important documents and a portrait of George Washington when the US Capitol building was set on fire.

13. The transcontinental railroad helped the _____ by allowing them to send letters and packages much faster.

Discover! SOCIAL STUDIES • GRADE 4 • CHAPTER 6 ASSESSMENT

121

Chapter Assessment Answer Key

1. B
2. D
3. B
4. C
5. True
6. True
7. False
8. False
9. True
10. 16, 500
11. France
12. Dolley Madison
13. postal service

122

Discover! SOCIAL STUDIES • GRADE 4 • CHAPTER 6 ASSESSMENT

Alternative Assessment

Project: Timeline

Create a timeline of the causes and effects of the War of 1812, Missouri Compromise, Monroe Doctrine, and transportation. Your student may need to do some research on the internet to find the years of some of the events. Make sure the events are in order on a timeline on a sheet of white paper. Draw a picture of each event above the event.

Project Requirements or Steps:

1. Research each topic below for the year in which it took place.

   - Missouri Compromise
   - Steamboat invention
   - Erie Canal
   - Transcontinental railroad built
   - Monroe Doctrine
   - US expansion wanted
   - War of 1812

2. On a sheet of paper, draw a line. Then add seven lines off of the center line to create a timeline.

3. Write each topic and information about each topic in the correct order on the timeline.

4. Draw a picture of each topic.

Discover! SOCIAL STUDIES • GRADE 4 • CHAPTER 6 ASSESSMENT

123

Alternative Assessment Rubric

Use the following rubric to grade your student's assessment.

	4	3	2	1	Points
Connection to the Chapter	The timeline is clearly connected to the chapter.	The timeline is connected to the chapter.	The timeline is somewhat connected to the chapter.	The timeline is not connected to the chapter.	
Creativity	The timeline is very creative and aesthetically appealing.	The timeline is creative and aesthetically appealing.	The timeline is somewhat creative and aesthetically appealing.	The timeline is not creative or aesthetically appealing.	
Information	The information or data is very accurate and easy to follow.	The information or data is accurate.	The information or data is somewhat accurate.	The information or data is not accurate.	
Grammar and Mechanics	There are no grammar and punctuation mistakes.	There are one or two grammar and punctuation mistakes.	There are several grammar and punctuation mistakes.	There are a distracting number of grammar and punctuation mistakes.	

Total Points _____/16

Average _____

124

Discover! SOCIAL STUDIES • GRADE 4 • CHAPTER 6 ASSESSMENT

Lesson Objectives

By the end of this lesson, your student will be able to:

- describe what happens when the majority of Electoral College votes are not won by any presidential candidate
- recognize that John Quincy Adams was the sixth president of the United States
- examine the problems some people had with John Quincy Adams's plans for the nation

Supporting Your Student

Read (John Quincy Adams)

The United States has currently and in the past had several different political parties. Have your student research to find out what happened to the Federalist Party and why. Have them make a three-column chart with information about past and current political parties in the United States. Label the columns with the political party name, a description of the party beliefs, and whether the party is still active.

Read (Electoral College)

The Electoral College plays a major role in presidential elections. To win the election, a candidate must receive at least 270 of the 538 possible electoral votes. The candidate with the most Electoral College votes wins the election. Have your student research to find out how many Electoral College votes each state gets. If they were a candidate, in which states would they spend most of their time and money campaigning?

Learning Styles

Auditory learners may enjoy a word of the day challenge. Challenge your student to use a tricky vocabulary word when speaking more times than you do in a given amount of time.

Visual learners may enjoy looking at the Electoral College map of the most recent presidential election. In what region of the country did the president win the most electoral votes? Or was it a mix?

Kinesthetic learners may enjoy the following: John Quincy Adams worked with the US Army Corp of Engineers as they led surveys for possible roads, canals, and railroads. Have your student research a famous US road, canal, or railroad and make a replica of one of them by using modeling clay, interlocking building blocks, or other crafting supplies.

Extension Activities

Electoral College

Print a blank map of the United States. Have your student research to find out how many Electoral College votes each state gets. Then have them write the number for each state inside of the state on the map. Have them research to find out why some states have more Electoral College votes than others.

Presidential Flipbook

Have your student create a flipbook of information about John Quincy Adams or another former president of your student's choice. The flipbook might include a biography, a timeline, a word search, the countries the president visited, true or false questions, or fun facts. The flipbook should help the reader understand who the former president was and how they did or did not help the United States.

Answer Key

Write *(Why do you think Adams decided to have his presidential portrait photographed instead of being painted like prior presidents?)*

Answers will vary. Possible answer: John Quincy Adams decided to have his presidential portrait photographed instead of painted because he was a progressive person who believed in using new discoveries and technology.

Write *(Some people say Adams was ahead of his time. Why do you think people say this?)*

Answers will vary. Possible answer: Adams was ahead of his time because he was a progressive person who was not afraid of progress and advancement. He was a dreamer and liked to use new technology and ideas alike to make the country a better place.

Show What You Know

1. D
2. A
3. B
4. B
5. Answers will vary. Possible answer: Many people had conflicting ideas on how to help and develop our country. Many people personally did not like John Quincy Adams. Some others believed his ideas cost too much money and were therefore unconstitutional.

Lesson Objectives

By the end of this lesson, your student will be able to:

- describe the presidential campaigns in 1828 for Andrew Jackson and John Quincy Adams
- identify the method Andrew Jackson wanted to use to fill government jobs

Supporting Your Student

Explore

Character traits are the aspects of a person's behavior and attitudes that make up that person's personality. Have your student think about the character traits of each president. If your student is struggling, they can make a Venn diagram to compare and contrast the presidents. When done, have them use the Venn diagram to write two paragraphs on how the presidents are alike and different.

Read (Presidential Campaigns of 1828)

As your student reads these sections, encourage them to highlight or underline unfamiliar words. Have them use the glossary or look up these words online to build their background knowledge. Encourage your student to use one new word in the correct context when speaking during the day.

After your student reads this section, ask them what could have been done to help Jackson and Adams have a more peaceful presidential campaign. Discuss your student's ideas with them.

Learning Styles

Auditory learners may enjoy a word of the day challenge. Challenge your student to use a tricky vocabulary word when speaking more times than you do in a given amount of time.

Visual learners may enjoy looking at pictures of America from 100 years ago. Have your student discuss changes from then to now.

Kinesthetic learners may enjoy researching and making a replica of the Erie Canal.

Extension Activities

Andrew Jackson on the $20 Bill

There has been some controversy about whether Andrew Jackson should be removed from the $20 bill. Andrew Jackson did not support using paper money. Why was he put on the $20 bill in the first place? Have your student research why Andrew Jackson appears on the $20 bill. Then have your student design a new $20 bill with a different person they think should appear on the bills.

Andrew Jackson

Andrew Jackson was an orphan. Have your student research to find out why. Did he have any relatives in his life as he grew up? Have your student write a report about his life as a child. Ask them to share their report with you.

Answer Key

Explore *(Research one of the countries that John Quincy Adams visited. What famous landmarks are there now that were there when Adams visited? Which one would you like to see in person?)*

Answers will vary. Possible answers: Notre Dame Cathedral, Mont Saint-Michel, and the Palace of Versailles

Write *(Why was the presidential campaign and election of 1828 significant? How were the Jackson and Adams campaigns alike and different?)*

Answers will vary. Possible answers: Jackson, a champion of the common public, won the election, and both candidates used personal attacks against their opponent. Jackson and Adams both accused the other of bad things during their campaigns. Jackson's accusations helped him to win the election.

Write *(Why were members of Congress against Adams and his ideas? Why did they agree with Jackson over Adams?)*

Answers will vary. Possible answers: Many members of Congress supported Jackson and disliked Adams. Many people preferred Jackson because he was a champion of the common people.

Take a Closer Look *(Adams's credibility and character were destroyed by accusations that were never confirmed to be true. How would our world be different had Adams won his reelection bid for president? How would history be rewritten?)*

Answers will vary. Possible answers: More of Adams's plans could have been successful, and he could have helped to build an interstate roads system and many canals. A national university could have been created.

Show What You Know

1. spoils
2. Jackson
3. Answers will vary. Possible answer: Andrew Jackson removed workers and replaced them with his supporters.
4. Answers will vary. Possible answer: During their campaigns, each candidate accused the other of some really bad things.

Lesson Objectives

By the end of this lesson, your student will be able to:

- summarize the key events in the history of the Cherokee after the Revolutionary War
- identify the main parts of the Indian Removal Act

Supporting Your Student

Online Connection

Make sure to help your student locate the official website of the museum. Guide your student through the different sections on the main menu navigation bar at the top of the page to find the exhibits. Guide your student through the exhibits and help them understand about the Cherokee way of life. In addition to the events described, have your student focus on the clothing, arts, and other aspects of culture.

Read (The Cherokee)

Explain to your student that the phrase the "Five Civilized Tribes" can be seen as an insult to the Cherokee way of life. The settlers assumed that the Cherokee were less advanced or inferior because they did not have the same lifestyle as the settlers did. Native Americans were not less advanced or less civilized. Your student may wonder why the Cherokee adopted the American culture. Explain that there were multiple reasons. The Cherokee may have liked some of the ideas but also wanted to avoid conflict with the powerful Americans. They thought that by trying to fit in and get along with the Americans, they might be able to keep their land—but it did not work as they were removed anyway.

Read (The Trail of Tears)

Support your student by showing them a map of the United States and pointing out information. Show the states in the Cherokee homeland (Georgia, North Carolina, South Carolina, Tennessee, and Alabama) and show where Oklahoma is. Discuss the distance between these states. Discuss how the lands are made up of mountainous terrain and how difficult travel would have been in historical times.

Learning Styles

Auditory learners may enjoy telling the story of the Cherokee in the style of traditional Native American storytellers. Your student may summarize the reading by playing the role of a Cherokee elder teaching about their ancestors.

Visual learners may enjoy researching images and videos showing more about Cherokee culture. An online search can discover many artists, works of art, tools, and weapons.

Kinesthetic learners may enjoy using action figures, dolls, stuffed animals, or puppets to act out the events in the text. Your student can act out three scenes: one of the Cherokee traditional ways, one of the signing of the Indian Removal Act, and one of the Trail of Tears.

Extension Activities

Create a Diorama

Your student can make a diorama depicting the Cherokee way of life or the events of removal. After making the diorama, your student can present the item and describe its meaning to family members in the manner of a museum docent. Dioramas can be made with simple materials such as paper, glue, scissors, and a shoebox. You can do an online search and show images to provide a model for your student.

Answer Key

Write *(Do you think that the Native Americans should have had to change their way of life to fit in with the settlers nearby? Why or why not?)*
Answers will vary. Possible responses may include references to more cooperative behaviors or making agreements together.

Practice *(Matching)*
1. Cherokee
2. Civilized Tribes
3. gold
4. Indian Removal Act
5. Andrew Jackson

Show What You Know
1. False
2. True
3. True
4. True
5. False
6. Answers will vary. Possible answers: forced relocation of the Cherokee to Oklahoma, the trip was made under harsh conditions, many people died from disease and exposure

Lesson Objectives

By the end of this lesson, your student will be able to:

- name Martin Van Buren as the eighth president of the United States
- recognize how the issue of slavery received more attention in the country while Van Buren was president
- describe the main goal of abolitionists

Supporting Your Student

Read *(Presidency of Martin Van Buren)*
Help your student understand the divide between the more industrialized North and the agrarian South. Your student should understand that the southern economy was based on large plantations of cash crops, such as cotton. The southern slaveholders were very wealthy, powerful, and influential. They wanted to keep their way of life even if it was cruel to enslaved African Americans.

Sidebar *(The Liberator)*
Help your student understand the vast difference in communication in the past compared to today. It was very difficult to spread information or organize people at this time, unlike with today's technology. At this time, very little information about the abolitionist movement could travel around until Garrison published his newspaper.

Learning Styles

Auditory learners may enjoy arguing both sides of a debate between William Lloyd Garrison and Martin Van Buren. Garrison could advocate for complete abolition of slavery, while Van Buren would explain why it's better to compromise.

Visual learners may enjoy making a graphic organizer to record information from the lesson.

Kinesthetic learners may enjoy making or tracing a map of the United States in 1836. They can color in slave states one color and free states another. Texas can be included to show how adding Texas would change the balance of power.

Extension Activities

Abolitionists Research
Learn more about how enslaved and free African Americans worked to help end slavery. Research a famous African American abolitionist. Suggestions include Frederick Douglass, Harriet Tubman, or Henry "Box" Brown. Each worked to end the practice of slavery and help enslaved people in different ways. Do further research into the Underground Railroad.

Answer Key

Write (*What rights do you think all human beings should have?*)

Answers will vary. Possible answers: clean drinking water, enough healthy food, health care and medicine

Write (*Do you think the court was right to side with the African men? Explain why.*)

Answers will vary. Discuss both yes and no possibilities and why. Then allow them to choose their response based on their personal thoughts resulting from the discussion.

Practice

1. *La Amistad*
2. Abolitionists
3. Martin Van Buren
4. Texas
5. *The Liberator*

Show What You Know

1. True
2. False
3. True
4. True
5. False
6. Answers will vary. Possible answers: *Amistad* revolt and trial, William Lloyd Garrison publishes *The Liberator*, Texas wants to join the US as a slave state

Lesson Objectives

By the end of this lesson, your student will review the following big ideas from Chapter 7.

- If no candidate gets a majority of the Electoral College votes, the decision goes to Congress. (Lesson 42)
- Andrew Jackson and John Quincy Adams ran very competitive campaigns during the 1828 election. (Lesson 43)
- The Indian Removal Act allowed Americans to force the Cherokee off their land and relocate them west of the Mississippi River. (Lesson 44)
- The issue of slavery received more attention in the country while President Van Buren was in office. Abolitionists were people who worked to end slavery. (Lesson 45)

Supporting Your Student

Online Connection

When your student is researching the Electoral College, stop often so they can take notes and discuss any questions that arise. You may want to compare past electoral college situations with current history to give your student the understanding that the Electoral College has been continuously evolving.

Practice (Vocabulary Activity)

While your student is working on this section, go back with them to previous lessons to discuss any word misunderstandings or confusion. Have your student read the sentences aloud to see which word or group of words makes the most sense.

Practice (Pros and Cons of the Electoral College)

Help your student set up a t-chart with pros and cons. Discuss which one they feel more knowledgeable about and encourage them to write an argument for that choice.

Practice (Venn Diagram)

Work with your student in filling in the Venn diagram for both groups. Remind your student that this will not be their opinion but just stating facts of each group's position on this issue.

Learning Styles

Auditory learners may enjoy listening to a story online told by a Native American expressing their feelings about opposing the Indian Removal Act. This story could also reflect upon the Trail of Tears.

Visual learners may enjoy finding pictures online of abolitionists and pictures of slaves working on plantations. They may want to print out some pictures to help with their writing.

Kinesthetic learners may enjoy writing and presenting a skit between Congress and a group of Native Americans that discusses the Indian Removal Act.

Extension Activities

Visit a Museum

Find a museum, either in your community or online, that highlights slavery during this time period and has displays of how communities looked at this time. If possible, visit the museum with your student. The museum displays may also include some readings by slaves or Indigenous peoples that will convey the way they felt during this time period.

Create a Timeline

Go back over the text with your student and highlight five key events that happened. Have your student write them each on an individual index card. Put the cards in order and have your student create a timeline.

Answer Key

Practice *(Vocabulary Activity)*

1. Transatlantic Slave Trade

2. abolitionist

3. Five Civilized Tribes

4. past

5. Trail of Tears

6. Indian Removal Act

Practice *(Pros and Cons of the Electoral College)*

Answers will vary. Possible answers: I believe that the Electoral College is bad because the people should vote for leaders directly. I think the Electoral College is good because it helps smaller states have an equal say in leaders.

Practice *(Venn Diagram)*

Answers will vary. Possible answers: Native Americans wanted to keep their land and way of life. Congress wanted to implement changes to benefit the new society by reorganizing land and the way industries were run. Both sides were fighting for what they believed in.

Quick Review

Refer to the statement your student circled in the Show What You Know section to self-assess their knowledge of the chapter concepts. Then to assist in determining if your student is ready to take the assessment, consider:

- Having your student explain the reasons why the Founding Fathers created the Electoral College.
- Having your student explain who Andrew Jackson and John Quincy Adams are.
- Having your student describe the purpose of the Indian Removal Act.
- Having your student explain the issue of slavery and who abolitionists are.

Discover! SOCIAL STUDIES • GRADE 4 • CHAPTER 7 ASSESSMENT

135

Chapter Assessment

Circle the correct answer for each question.

1. True or False   John Quincy Adams was the first president who was a son of a president.

2. True or False   John Quincy Adams did not serve in the administrations of all the presidents that came before him.

3. True or False   In the election of 1828, Jackson defeated Adams by an electoral vote of 178 to 83.

4. Why was the election of 1828 unique?

   A. Nominations were no longer made by Congressional caucuses but by conventions and the state legislatures.

   B. There were more than two candidates in the running.

   C. The votes had to be recounted.

5. Who signed the Indian Removal Act into law on May 28, 1830?

   A. President George Washington

   B. President Andrew Jackson

   C. President Harry S. Truman

6. Slavery formed a cornerstone of the _____.

   A. colonists

   B. Democratic Party

   C. British Empire

Fill in the blank for each question.

7. An _____ is one who works to end the practice of slavery.

8. The _____ was the forced march of the Cherokee people from their homeland to the Oklahoma Territory.

9. _____ influenced every aspect of colonial thought and culture.

Answer the following question in complete sentences.

10. Write a short paragraph about the Trail of Tears. What does it mean and what impact did it have on the Native American society?

Chapter Assessment Answer Key

1. True
2. False
3. True
4. A
5. B
6. C
7. abolitionist
8. Trail of Tears
9. Slavery
10. Answers will vary. Possible answers: The Trail of Tears was when the US government forced Native Americans to move from their homelands in the Southern United States to Indian Territory in Oklahoma.

Alternative Assessment

Project: Timeline

Create a timeline for one of the groups you compared using the Venn diagram in the worktext. Identify the goals of each group and details about their position on the Indian Removal Act. Then put these events in order on the timeline.

Project Requirements or Steps:

1. Write down the reasons the group you chose wanted the Indian Removal Act.

2. Number the events in the order from 1 (first) to 5 (last).

3. Draw a line across a piece of white paper.

4. Write the events in order below the line.

5. Write the year each event occurred above each event.

Using your timeline, write a paragraph that describes the events and when these events took place.

Alternative Assessment Rubric

Use the following rubric to grade your student's assessment.

	4	**3**	**2**	**1**	**Points**
Connection to the Chapter	The timeline is clearly connected to the chapter.	The timeline is connected to the chapter.	The timeline is somewhat connected to the chapter.	The timeline is not connected to the chapter.	
Creativity	The timeline is very creative and aesthetically appealing.	The timeline is creative and aesthetically appealing.	The timeline is somewhat creative and aesthetically appealing.	The timeline is not creative or aesthetically appealing.	
Information	The information or data is very accurate and easy to follow.	The information or data is accurate.	The information or data is somewhat accurate.	The information or data is not accurate.	
Grammar and Mechanics	There are no grammar and punctuation mistakes.	There are one or two grammar and punctuation mistakes.	There are several grammar and punctuation mistakes.	There are a distracting number of grammar and punctuation mistakes.	

Total Points _____/16

Average _____

Discover! SOCIAL STUDIES • GRADE 4 • CHAPTER 7 ASSESSMENT

139

Lesson Objectives

By the end of this lesson, your student will be able to:

- describe how canals were essential in beginning to connect the eastern and western United States
- evaluate supply and demand, using steamboat companies as an example
- analyze the role railroads played in connecting cities and helping them grow

Supporting Your Student

Read *(Canals in the 1800s)*
Read the text with your student and discuss what they already knew about canals and what is interesting to them. Have them go back to the text and stop often to understand the development of canals.

Read *(Railroads Connected Cities)*
Read the text with your student and have them stop often to explain what they are learning. You could ask, "Have you ever been on a railroad or train?" or "Do you remember seeing people or goods traveling on the railroad in books you have read or movies you have seen?"

Read *(Steamboats, Supply, and Demand)*
To further explain the basic concepts of supply and demand, read *The Lorax* by Dr. Seuss. Discuss the book and make connections to the characters and products with the concepts of supply and demand.

Learning Styles

Auditory learners may enjoy listening to recordings from the building of the Erie Canal or the first railroad builders.

Visual learners may enjoy finding pictures of different railroad companies in the country and make note of their similarities and differences.

Kinesthetic learners may enjoy singing "I've Been Working on the Railroad" with props to explain the song.

Extension Activities

Create a Railroad
Using legos or cardboard, Have your student create a railroad station or model train in the railroad station using legos or cardboard. Ask them questions about what the railroad station will help the people of the community do.

Supply and Demand
Have your student design a storyboard that tells the story of supply and demand. Have your student choose a product they will enjoy drawing and writing about, such as candy. Ask your student where the product starts. What ingredients are used to make the product? Where do those come from? Where does the product end up?

Answer Key

Show What You Know

1. D
2. E
3. B
4. C
5. A
6. False
7. True
8. A <u>railroad</u> is a track or set of tracks made of steel rails along which passenger and freight trains run. The railroad industry played an important role in building <u>cities</u> across the country. People could resettle to cities where <u>factory</u> demand for labor meant employment. The building of railroads opened the way for the <u>settlement</u> of the West.

Lesson Objectives

By the end of this lesson, your student will be able to:

- identify the positive and negative outcomes of living in a city
- explain the connection between agriculture and the South and identify the reasons crops grew well there
- describe the characteristics of a plantation
- describe the differences between living on a small farm and a plantation
- explain how jobs located in cities and ports, such as blacksmithing, were important to farms

Supporting Your Student

Read (Living in a City)

Discuss with your student what life was like in the cities during this time. Ask them what the connection is between agriculture and the South. Ask, "Why did crops grow better there?" and "How much work do you think it was to distribute these farm products to other cities in the country?"

Read (Agriculture in the South)

When your student is reading about plantations and farming in the South, be sure they are clear about the different regions and why growing crops may be more successful in the South. Ask your student how they think those in slavery felt in this part of the country, working in the fields in bad weather or in poor conditions.

Read (City and Port Jobs)

When reading this passage with your student, ask questions such as "What do you think a dockworker did?," "Do you know anyone who is a blacksmith or cooper?," and "How did these jobs help farmers?"

Write (Name a job held by someone working at a port. Name a job held by someone working in a city that helped farmers.)

Before answering questions, review with your student about city life during this time, jobs in ports, and jobs that helped farmers.

Learning Styles

Auditory learners may enjoy listening to a story told by a plantation worker about their experiences.

Visual learners may enjoy organizing pictures of different jobs and using words that describe their jobs under each picture.

Kinesthetic learners may enjoy acting out a day at a port and working on a dock loading or unloading goods as a job. They can use props to represent goods.

Extension Activities

Cities in the Colonies

Help your student go online and read stories about a particular city in the colonies such as Philadelphia or New Orleans. Talk with them about how these cities contributed to the nation's economic growth and discuss what life was like in this area.

Virtual Museum Tour

Find a virtual museum (or a local one if possible) that you can visit with your student that depicts an aspect of the growth in cities. For example, the growth in transportation over time.

Answer Key

Write *(Why was the South ideal for agriculture? What is a plantation, and what was it used for? What kind of people worked there, and what were they growing?)*

The warm climate and fertile soil made the South the more ideal place for agriculture. Individual pieces of land were called plantations, which were known for growing cotton, rice, and tobacco. Wealthy plantation owners used enslaved people to grow and harvest their crops. They exported their goods to the North and to Europe through port cities.

Write *(Name a job held by someone working at a port. Name a job held by someone working in a city that helped farmers.)*

Port—dock loading and unloading; City—cooper, blacksmith, carpenter

Practice

Answers will vary. Possible answer: Being a cooper involves making wooden barrels and casks from staved timber. To be a cooper, you need to be able to measure, cut, and shape wood accurately. It is still a job today.

Show What You Know

1. True
2. False
3. True
4. True
5. False
6. Answers will vary. Possible answer: The North had more big cities and smaller farms. The South had big plantations, soil that was ideal for farming, and few big cities. Both the North and the South had shipping ports to export goods.

LESSON 49
Technological Advances

Lesson Objectives

By the end of this lesson, your student will be able to:

- analyze the reasons manufacturing mostly occurred in the Northeast
- identify advancements in technology that helped improve work on farms and in cities
- describe why inventors would need patents to protect the inventions they make
- evaluate the costs and benefits of technology

Supporting Your Student

Take a Closer Look (Chicago)

Help your student understand the distinct parts of the commerce system that developed around Chicago. First, farmers sent raw materials like crops or animals into the city. Then, the factories processed the raw materials into goods, such as canned vegetables or meat. Finally, the finished products were shipped out to grocery stores.

Explore

Your student may wonder if workplaces are still dangerous or if children still work at a young age. Explain the benefits of child labor laws, workplace safety laws, and unions.

Read (The Patent Office)

Explain the rights of inventors to copyright or patent their inventions. Use the example of an artist who creates a character who is popular in an animated movie. The artist can license the character's image to companies that make hats and T-shirts. Then the artist receives a small royalty on each sale. This system allows everyone to do business and make profits while protecting the original inventor.

Learning Styles

Auditory learners may enjoy recording themselves telling the story of a factory worker. They can summarize factory life by including information from the lesson.

Visual learners may enjoy viewing or drawing diagrams of a factory.

Kinesthetic learners may enjoy creating a model of a factory by using building blocks and crafting supplies.

Extension Activities

The Steam Engine

Your student can research the foundational invention to the Industrial Revolution: the steam engine. Have them begin by learning the early invention by Thomas Newcomen and the improvements made by James Watt. Then have them research the use of the engine in locomotives, ships, and factories.

Video Quest

Have your student search for videos of agricultural machines at work. Have them look for a tractor, thresher, and combine. Then have them search for videos showing factory processes. Tell your student to start with the powered loom and then find any video showing an assembly line. This activity will help your student visualize the systems.

Answer Key

Write *(Would you have liked to work in a factory every day? Why or why not?)*
Answers will vary. Your student should demonstrate an understanding of working in a factory during the Industrial Revolution.

Write *(Since machines could do the work for people, what do you think all of the farm workers did after these inventions became common?)*
Answers will vary. Possible answers: They stayed on the farm to work machines. They moved away to find work in the cities. They learned machine repair as a trade.

Show What You Know

1. Industrial Revolution
2. loom
3. patent
4. combine
5. factory
6. southern, Northeast
7. Answers will vary. Possible answers: The smoke caused pollution. Children had to work long hours. Southern plantations continued to utilize enslaved people.
8. True
9. False
10. True
11. True
12. True

Lesson Objectives

By the end of this lesson, your student will be able to:

- describe how the United States Postal Service developed
- describe how a telegraph works
- identify examples of businesses that used the telegraph

Supporting Your Student

Read *(The US Postal Service)*

Your student likely understands the use of letters for official documents, bills, and other paper-based communication. However, people rarely exchange friendly letters via post anymore. Describe the postal delivery as it was a generation ago where personal communication was more by letter. Explain how the telephone, then email, then social media have changed this cultural norm.

Take a Closer Look *(Morse Code)*

Help your student experience Morse Code to understand how the telegraph worked. Use any device that makes a sound and determine how to make a short sound for a dot and a longer sound for a dash. Take turns sending messages back and forth that spell out a word.

Read *(It's a Small World)*

Assist your student by explaining this metaphorical concept. The actual distance between people did not change, but the way it was perceived did. Before the Industrial Revolution, contact outside your town was rare. You did not have access to products outside the general store or what was made by local artisans. You would rarely hear news from other towns or states. Contrast this to today's instant communication and delivery of items.

Learning Styles

Auditory learners may enjoy recording a summary of the advancements in communication.

Visual learners may enjoy watching videos to see how the telegraph and its cables were invented and operated.

Kinesthetic learners may enjoy trying out Morse Code by tapping dots and dashes to form words.

Extension Activities

Industrial Revolutions Research

Your student can research the third and fourth Industrial Revolutions. They will find out about the electrical/digital-based advances from the third Industrial Revolution that shape much of the world today. Then your student will discover that we are in the midst of the fourth Industrial Revolution. Smart technologies and the internet are changing life right now. For further extension, make sure your student makes connections between the inventions in the 1800s and the ones we use today.

Follow the Package

If you order any items that have tracking, your student can follow along with the tracking information. This will show them how the postal service moves packages across the country and world. Plot the route on a map.

Answer Key

Write *(What do you think people meant when they expressed "the world is getting smaller"?)*
Answers will vary. Possible answers: Communication made it easier to talk to people far away. The telegraph connected parts of the world. People living in another state didn't seem that far away anymore because you could talk to them easily.

Show What You Know

1. B
2. C
3. B
4. A, B, C
5. A
6. False
7. True
8. False
9. True
10. True
11. Answers will vary. Possible answers:
   standard rates/routes, well mapped routes,
   regular schedule

Lesson Objectives

By the end of this lesson, your student will review the following big ideas from Chapter 8.

- Railroads and canals allowed people and goods to travel between cities faster. (Lesson 47)
- Different ways of life developed in cities and on farms. (Lesson 48)
- Technological advances made eastern cities centers of industry. (Lesson 49)
- Advances such as the postal service and telegraph made communication faster. (Lesson 50)

Supporting Your Student

Play

Engage your student in a comparison of city and farm living during the 1800s before playing. Ask your student to tell you three things about life that were different in rural and urban settings in that time period. Then your student can use the information to help develop the play.

Practice (City Life and Farm Life)

Your student will likely be able to determine elements of life that are unique to farms compared to urban centers. Help your student figure out the areas of commonality that should be represented with the center of the Venn diagram. For example, advancements in technology and faster communication affected farmers as well as city dwellers.

Practice (Positives and Negatives)

Your student may consider advancement in technology as a positive change. Explain that advancement in technology often has positive effects but also always has some consequences. Sometimes the consequences can be negative.

Learning Styles

Auditory learners may enjoy delivering a speech comparing the positives and negatives of the advancements in technology.

Visual learners may enjoy observing pictures or videos of the new inventions from the 1800s.

Kinesthetic learners may enjoy drawing diagrams or building models of the inventions.

Extension Activities

How Do They Make It?

Have your student select two to three products that they use in everyday life. Then have them research the way the product is manufactured in a factory. Use online web and video searches to find out the steps in the manufacturing process. Watch how the item is made. Compare the process to those used before the Industrial Revolution.

Letter Home

Have your student perform a simulation pretending they are a former farmworker who has moved to the city to find work in the 1800s. They must incorporate information from the chapter such as railroads, canals, factories, and developments in agriculture. Make sure your student describes the conditions that workers faced in this time period.

Answer Key

Write *(How are canals and railroads similar? How are they different?)*

Answers may vary. Possible answers: Canals and railroads both made it easier to transport products. Canals can only be built where there are already waterways.

Practice *(Vocabulary Drawings)*

Drawings may vary. Check your student's drawings to ensure they have a firm understanding of each vocabulary word.

Practice *(City Life and Farm Life)*

Answers may vary. Possible answers:

City life: had factories, ports, railroads, and pollution; was more common in the northeast

Farm life: had plantations, agriculture, cash crops, and good soil; was more common in the southeast

Both: had new technology, traded goods and products, benefited from faster communication

Practice *(Positives and Negatives)*

Answers may vary. Possible answers:

Positives: makes more products, faster travel, faster communication, more wealth

Negatives: child labor, unsafe workplaces, pollution, diseases

Quick Review

Refer to the statement your student circled in the Show What You Know section to self-assess their knowledge of the chapter concepts. Then to assist in determining if your student is ready to take the assessment, consider:

- Having your student describe at least three inventions that made American workers more productive in the 1800s.
- Having your student explain the inventions covered in this chapter.
- Having your student explain if they would like to work in an 1800s factory.

Chapter Assessment

Choose the correct answer for each question.

1. What was the most important effect of canals?

A. Wealthy people could use sailboats for entertainment.

B. Steamships could transport products from city to city.

C. People could move if they wanted a new home state.

2. How did steamboats change the balance of supply and demand for goods?

A. Many people wanted to buy steamboats.

B. Steam ruined many products when shipped.

C. It was easier to supply products because the steamboats shipped them faster.

3. What region of the country became the leading center of industry?

A. northeast

B. southeast

C. west

4. What document gives inventors the right to make money from their own inventions?

A. patent

B. constitution

C. legal clerk

5. What do the tractor, combine, and cotton gin have in common?

A. They all were powered by electricity.

B. They all made farmwork more productive.

C. They were used mainly in port cities.

Discover! SOCIAL STUDIES • GRADE 4 • CHAPTER 8 ASSESSMENT

151

Use the words from the Word Bank to complete the questions below.

Word Bank: loom   plantation   post office   railroad   telegraph

6. A _____ is a large farm where enslaved people were forced to work.

7. The _____ made communication instantaneous.

8. Improvements to the _____ made mail delivery more reliable.

9. The powered _____ was used in mills to make cloth from cotton.

10. New cities were built at stops along the _____ route.

Answer the following questions in complete sentences.

11. How did the railroad and canals change life in America? Describe two important changes.

....
....
....
....
....
....
....

12. Was the rapid industrialization of America a positive or negative development? Explain two pros and two cons to the changes that occurred during the 1800s.

....
....
....
....
....
....
....

Chapter Assessment Answer Key

1. B
2. C
3. A
4. A
5. B
6. plantation
7. telegraph
8. post office
9. loom
10. railroad
11. Answers may vary. Possible answers: Canals and railroads connected people. Goods and products could be shipped faster and further. The North became industrialized.
12. Answers may vary. Possible answers: There were many new products. People could communicate. Children had to work in bad conditions. There was pollution and disease.

Discover! SOCIAL STUDIES • GRADE 4 • CHAPTER 8 ASSESSMENT

153

Alternative Assessment

Project: Advancements of the Industrial Revolution Collage

In this project, you will create a collage relating to a topic from the chapter.

Project Requirements or Steps:

A collage is a creative collection of photographs or drawings. Follow the steps below to create your collage.

1. Choose five or more important inventions.

2. Print, draw, or cut out images of each invention.

3. Arrange them in an interesting pattern.

4. Make a colorful background from poster board or other similar material.

5. Attach the invention images to the background.

6. Write two important facts about each invention on note cards.

7. Present your collage and read the important facts to an audience such as your instructor and family members.

Alternative Assessment Rubric

Use the following rubric to grade your student's assessment.

	4	3	2	1	Points
Connection to the Chapter	The collage is clearly connected to the chapter.	The collage is connected to the chapter.	The collage is somewhat connected to the chapter.	The collage is not connected to the chapter.	
Creativity	The collage is very creative and visually appealing.	The collage is creative and visually appealing.	The collage is somewhat creative or visually appealing.	The collage is not creative or visually appealing.	
Organization	The collage is very organized.	The collage is organized.	The collage is somewhat organized.	The collage is disorganized.	
Background	The background is very neat, colorful, and meaningful.	The background is neat, colorful, and meaningful.	The background is colorful.	The background is plain or sloppy.	

Total Points _____/16

Average _____

Discover! SOCIAL STUDIES • GRADE 4 • CHAPTER 8 ASSESSMENT

155

Lesson Objectives

By the end of this lesson, your student will be able to:

- identify the laws created by Mexico that people in Texas had to follow
- identify the reason that Texans ended up fighting a war against Mexico
- summarize the key points of the agreement for Texas's independence from Mexico

Supporting Your Student

Read *(Settling in Texas)*

Help your student understand the sparse population of Texas at this time. It may be difficult for students living in urban areas today to imagine the vast amount of open land in the past. The migration of Americans into Texas greatly changed the population density and demographics of the region.

Read *(Santa Anna Becomes President)*

Explain that Santa Anna attempted to concentrate power in his own hands rather than following the Mexican Constitution. He ruled as a dictator who enforced his own policies. Santa Anna was popular with some people because he showed strength and patriotism. However, many people viewed him negatively. His leadership left people with mixed opinions.

Practice

Prepare your student by explaining the short essay questions require facts from the reading and inferences. Your student should attempt to infer conclusions from the information and their own reasoning ability.

Learning Styles

Auditory learners may enjoy recording a debate between Santa Anna and Stephen F. Austin about who should control Texas.

Visual learners may enjoy using videos, maps, and images to construct the story of the War of Texas Independence.

Kinesthetic learners may enjoy creating a model of the Alamo or the Lone Star Flag.

Extension Activities

Six Flags Over Texas

Texas has a complex political history. The Texas state house displays six flags to symbolize the series of governments that controlled Texas in succession. Have your student research the six different time periods of Texas history and plot them on a timeline.

Texas Geography

Have your student take a deep dive into the political, cultural, and physical geography of Texas. Have your student research the state of Texas. Make sure they find information relating to:

- Geography: Austin, Houston, the Alamo, San Jacinto, the Rio Grande river
- State symbols: state motto, state flag, etc.
- Culture: traditional foods, music, arts

Your student can create a collage or poster about Texas to show what they learned.

Answer Key

Write *(Why do you think that Texans are proud of the events at the Alamo?)*

Answers will vary. Possible answers: They admire the bravery of the soldiers. It is a symbol of fighting for Texas. They honor those who gave their lives in the battle.

Practice

1. True
2. True
3. False
4. False
5. True

Show What You Know

1. B
2. C
3. D
4. A
5. D
6. Answers will vary. Possible answers: American settlers outnumbered Mexican citizens. The Texans might want to join the United States.
7. Answers will vary. Possible answers: The Texans were inspired by the bravery of the soldiers. The Texans wanted revenge for the defeat.

Lesson Objectives

By the end of this lesson, your student will be able to:

- recognize why the United States wanted to annex California to the country
- identify the main events that led to war between the United States and Mexico
- recognize how advancements in weaponry can provide advantages during a war
- identify the main events during the Mexican-American War that led to the United States' victory

Supporting Your Student

Read *(The War Begins)*

Explain to your student that weapons in the past were much less accurate and effective than those we may think of today. Any newer weapons would make a large difference in the outcome of a war because older versions took a long time to load and shot inaccurately. The production of newer weapons in the United States was an important factor in the battles' outcomes.

Read *(The Mexican Cession)*

Make sure to clarify the difference between the terms *cession*, *session*, and *secession* as needed in this and future lessons. A *cession* in this lesson means the giving of land from one country to another. In later lessons, your student may use the term *secession*, which means a state withdrawing from a country.

Write *(Describe two or more of the reasons the United States and Mexico fought this war.)*

Help your student understand that the causes of a large war are often complex and varied instead of there being one single cause. In this case, there were numerous contributory causes. Many Americans were still angry over the events at the Alamo, and many Mexicans still considered Texas rightfully part of Mexico. Settlers in California rebelled against Mexico, and Mexican leaders believed the United States would encourage other rebellions. Additionally, the American belief in Manifest Destiny played a role. Your student can also name the border dispute at the Rio Grande

that started the actual fight but must also understand the other causes which caused the overall conflict.

Learning Styles

Auditory learners may enjoy recording themselves explaining a summary of the events of the Mexican-American War.

Visual learners may enjoy viewing various paintings, images, and videos about the Mexican-American War.

Kinesthetic learners may enjoy drawing a map of the United States and Mexico and moving simulated troops to the locations of battles to reenact the war.

Extension Activities

Biography

Have your student choose one of the important people featured in the events of the Mexican-American War. Have them look up information using two to four online sources and write a biography summarizing their important achievements:

- James Polk
- Zachary Taylor
- Winfield Scott
- Antonio López de Santa Anna

Geography of the Mexican Cession

Have your student create a mixed-use political and physical map of the lands of the Mexican Cession. Have them label the political boundaries of the states and mark important cities. Have them draw in mountains, deserts, and other important landforms as well as all major rivers and other waterways.

Answer Key

Practice

1. True
2. True
3. False
4. False
5. True

Write *(Describe two or more of the reasons the United States and Mexico fought this war.)*

Answers may vary. Possible answers: the American belief in Manifest Destiny, many people in Mexico and the United States wanted revenge on Santa Anna, border disputes in Texas

Show What You Know

1. F
2. D
3. B
4. A
5. C
6. E
7. 3
8. 1
9. 4
10. 2

Lesson Objectives

By the end of this lesson, your student will be able to:

- identify the events that helped cause California's population to greatly increase
- examine how the Gold Rush affected the supply and demand of products in California
- describe how the increase in population affected law and order in California

Supporting Your Student

Read (Migration to California)

Connect the Fugitive Slave Act to the migration of both free and enslaved African Americans to California. Since California was not yet a state under US federal law, fugitive slaves were somewhat safer there than even in most northern states.

Remind your student about the facts they know about the Mexican-American War. Your student should remember that Mexico ceded a large tract of land to the United States at the end of the war. Additionally, Mexico gave up all claims to the northern part of California (Alta California). You can point out familiar city names such as San Francisco and Sacramento to show how these cities grew large during the Gold Rush and are still important today.

Read (Mining for Gold)

Help your student understand that the 1849 prospectors used only simple equipment to mine for gold compared to today. We now have large-scale industrial mining equipment that creates enormous mines. You can research images of modern mining techniques to show your student for a comparison.

Learning Styles

Auditory learners may enjoy recording a summary of the events of the Gold Rush. The recording can be done in the style of an entertaining podcast that recounts the events as an exciting story.

Visual learners may enjoy watching videos of how gold is mined and researching images from the Gold Rush.

Kinesthetic learners may enjoy sketching a diagram of the gold mining process or acting out the process with hands-on materials.

Extension Activities

Precious Metals

Have your student research a variety of precious metals such as gold, silver, platinum, copper, and tin. Your student can find out what the metal looks like and how it is mined. Then have them make a list of important ways each metal can be used in products.

Go Gem Mining

Many vacation spots have simulated gem mining activities complete with a water run, sluice, and pans. Your student can also recreate this activity with dirt, sand, backyard rocks, and any other easy to find items. Alternatively, they can order gem mining bags online. Use a video search to see how the activity works.

Answer Key

Write *(What effect do you think the vast increase in people had in California? Write down two to three difficulties people might face in a territory when so many people move in so fast.)*
Answers will vary. Possible answers: There may not be enough houses to live in or stores to buy things. The public services like police, fire, and government won't be big enough to handle all the needs. The people may come into conflict as they all want the same gold.

Show What You Know

1. C
2. C
3. A, B, C
4. B
5. A
6. True
7. False
8. False
9. False
10. True
11. Answers will vary. Possible answers: Some people gained lots of money to improve their lives. California became a free state. Most people did not find much gold. Crime increased.

Lesson Objectives

In this lesson, your student will review the following big ideas from Chapter 9.

- Many Americans moved into the Texas territory controlled by Mexico. War broke out, and the Texans eventually gained independence. (Lesson 52)
- Border disputes between Texans and Mexico later flared up into a larger conflict. The United States won a swift victory in the Mexican-American War. (Lesson 53)
- Mexico gave up large amounts of land to the United States. The California Gold Rush caused a mass migration of prospectors into California. (Lesson 54)

Supporting Your Student

Practice *(Three's a Crowd)*

Before starting the activity, help your student with the process that goes into creating an answer to this activity. Your student should be looking for a pair of words that fit a similar theme or topic and making sure the remaining word does not fit that theme. The second part of the activity is designed for your student to explain and record their process.

Practice *(Compare Texas and California Settlers)*

Use this activity to help your student analyze the differences between the events in California and in Texas. The migrants to Texas were overwhelmingly from other US states near Texas. They wanted to replicate a similar lifestyle to that of the plantations, large farms, and ranches in the American South. California's settlers were far more diverse and included Europeans, Chinese, South Americans, free African Americans, and people who escaped slavery in the South.

Practice *(Making an Argument)*

Focus your student on the difference between academic argument and simple persuasion. Persuasion can use emotional pleas or powerful rhetoric to accomplish the goal of changing someone's mind. Academic argument shares some general principles, but is far different. The argument is based on laying out a thesis or claim and supporting it with facts from various credible sources. Make sure your student uses evidence to support or refute the claim.

Learning Styles

Auditory learners may enjoy recording a "breaking news" segment dramatizing the events of one of the lessons in the chapter.

Visual learners may enjoy creating a slideshow of important images from the chapter.

Kinesthetic learners may enjoy making maps of the major battle and conflict locations and the Mexican Cession.

Extension Activities

Manifest Destiny

Have your student consider the points of view of Native Americans, U.S. President Polk, and Mexican citizens. Each of these groups had a different point of view about Manifest Destiny. Your students should write two to three sentences for each group explaining how they likely viewed the idea that the United States should stretch from the Atlantic to the Pacific.

Mapping the United States in 1850

Have your student create a political map of the United States showing state borders. Choose three colored pencils to shade in the three major components of US territory circa 1850: the 13 colonies, the Louisiana Purchase, and the Mexican Cession.

Answer Key

Practice *(Three's a Crowd!)*

1. prospectors
2. Rio Grande
3. Tennessee
4. Sutter
5. Alamo

Write *(Choose two of the word sets above. Write an explanation of how you arrived at the answer. Include what the matching pair had in common and why the third word did not fit.)*
Answers will vary. Possible answer: The Alamo and the Nueces River were sources of conflict around the Texas border. Prospectors looked for gold in California.

Practice *(Compare Texas Settlers and California Settlers)*
Answers will vary. Possible answers:

Texas Settlers: border conflict, owned large farms

California Settlers: looking for gold, European, Chinese, mostly young men

Both: from the US states, conflict with Santa Anna

Practice *(Making an Argument)*
Answers will vary. Possible answers:

- The claim is true. Santa Anna wanted too much power and brutally killed many Americans. But the U.S. believed they could move west even though Mexico owned the land. Both were at fault.
- The claim is false. Mexico already claimed the land, so the United States had no right to it.
- The claim is false. Mexico started hostilities by passing laws against Texans and sending troops into Texas.

Quick Review

Refer to the statement your student circled in the Show What You Know section to self-assess their knowledge of the chapter concepts. Then to assist in determining if your student is ready to take the assessment, consider:

- Asking your student to show how the borders of Mexico changed over time.
- Ensuring your student can differentiate between the Texas War for Independence and the Mexican-American War. These conflicts have some overlap in people, places, and causes, but your student should be able to explain the differences.
- Asking your student to explain how the Gold Rush had positive and negative effects on various people.

Chapter Assessment

Circle the correct answer.

1. Why did many Texans and Mexicans oppose Santa Anna?

   A. He tried to take too much power for himself.

   B. He was not born in Mexico.

   C. He was weak and feared battle.

2. Which of the following best describes Texas? Select all that apply.

   A. a US state

   B. formerly part of Mexico

   C. formerly its own country

3. What event convinced most Mexicans they had lost to the United States?

   A. US troops took Mexico City.

   B. Californians kept all the gold.

   C. Santa Anna captured the Alamo.

4. What was the outcome of the Treaty of Guadalupe-Hidalgo?

   A. Texans were freed from prison.

   B. Mexico ceded land to the United States.

   C. The Alamo was rebuilt.

5. What was a negative outcome of the Gold Rush?

   A. California wrote a Constitution.

   B. Mexico ceded land.

   C. There was lots of crime.

Discover! SOCIAL STUDIES • GRADE 4 • CHAPTER 9 ASSESSMENT

165

Answer the following questions in complete sentences.

6. The Texans used the rallying cry "Remember the Alamo" to motivate their troops—even though they lost the battle at that location. What happened at the Alamo, and why did it motivate Texans?

....

....

....

....

....

....

7. There were numerous results of the California Gold Rush. Describe three of the effects.

....

....

....

....

....

....

Chapter Assessment Answer Key

1. A

2. A, B, C

3. A

4. B

5. C

6. Answers will vary. Possible answers: Texans were proud of the troops' bravery. Texans wanted revenge for the deaths.

7. Answers will vary. Possible answers: Hundreds of thousands of people moved to California. California became a state. Because there was little government enforcement, crime increased.

Discover! SOCIAL STUDIES • GRADE 4 • CHAPTER 9 ASSESSMENT

167

Alternative Assessment

Project: Advertisement for Texas or California

Advertisements are notices or announcements in a public medium promoting a product, service, or event designed to persuade you to take action.

Project Requirements or Steps:

For this project, create a print advertisement to convince an audience to move to Texas or California. Include the following elements in the advertisement:

- Headline about the topic
- A tagline or slogan related to the topic
- Key information about the topic
- A visual or graphic element illustrating the topic
- Color to catch the eye of the audience

Alternative Assessment Rubric

Use the following rubric to grade your student's assessment.

	4	3	2	1	Points
Connection to the Chapter	The advertisement is clearly connected to the chapter.	The advertisement is connected to the chapter.	The advertisement is somewhat connected to the chapter.	The advertisement is not connected to the chapter.	
Creativity	The advertisement is very creative and aesthetically appealing.	The advertisement is creative and aesthetically appealing.	The advertisement is somewhat creative and aesthetically appealing.	The advertisement is not creative or aesthetically appealing.	
Information	The information or data is very accurate and easy to follow.	The information or data is accurate.	The information or data is somewhat accurate.	The information or data is not accurate.	
Grammar and Mechanics	There are no grammar and punctuation mistakes.	There are one or two grammar and punctuation mistakes.	There are several grammar and punctuation mistakes.	There are a distracting number of grammar and punctuation mistakes.	

Total Points _____/16

Average _____

Discover! SOCIAL STUDIES • GRADE 4 • CHAPTER 9 ASSESSMENT

169

Compromise of 1850

Lesson Objectives

By the end of this lesson, your student will be able to:

- compare and contrast the viewpoints and actions of Taylor, Calhoun, and Clay toward the issue of slavery
- identify the creators of the Compromise of 1850
- state the purpose of the Compromise of 1850

Supporting Your Student

Explore

For this section, think of some real-life examples of compromises that you have made with others to share with your student. Try to share examples that involve other family members or people that your student would know. By your sharing real-world examples of compromise, your student will be able to gain a deeper understanding of what a compromise is and how they are used to solve conflicts.

Practice

For this activity, assist your student by giving them a highlighter and rereading the text from the Read "What Was the Compromise of 1850?" section. Encourage them to find and highlight the phrases to discover the words to fill in each blank.

Show What You Know

For the True or False section of the assessment, you can support your student by underlining key information in each sentence that makes the statement true or false. For example, in question 7, you may underline the last three words of the sentence to help students to pay close attention to those words (i.e., The Fugitive Slave Act made sure runaway slaves living in free states could remain free).

Learning Styles

Auditory learners may enjoy listening to the speeches from the debates surrounding the Compromise of 1850 or other speeches from that time period.

Visual learners may enjoy viewing primary documents from the Compromise of 1850. Laws, speeches, and the bills passed during the Compromise of 1850 can be found online by searching the key phrase "Henry Clay Compromise of 1850 primary documents."

Kinesthetic learners may enjoy hosting a debate with family and friends over a topic they are passionate about.

Extension Activities

Debate Detour

Have your student search for a local debate team and attend one of their debate meets. If you cannot find a local meet, many high schools have debate teams that practice regularly. This would be a fun way for your student to see a formal debate and hear what it may have been like for the politicians who were debating over the Compromise of 1850.

Southern Symbols

Have your student take a look into some of the symbols from the South during the time leading up to the Civil War. Many of these symbols are frowned upon today. Educate your student on what the symbols mean and why they are not used anymore.

Answer Key

Explore
A compromise is reached if Eli holds the leash for the first half of the walk and Mike holds the leash for the second half of the walk.

Practice
1. North
2. South
3. illegal
4. California
5. Fugitive

Show What You Know
1. D
2. A
3. C
4. B
5. False
6. True
7. False
8. False
9. True
10. Answers will vary. Possible answer: The northerners wanted to see the new territories become free of slavery. The southerners wanted slavery to expand to the new territories.
11. Answers will vary. Possible answer: The Compromise of 1850 was a fair compromise because it gave the northerners and southerners some of what they wanted. California became a free state, which made the North happy. New Mexico and Utah territories were open to slavery, which made the South happy.

Slavery

Lesson Objectives

By the end of this lesson, your student will be able to:

- describe how slaves lived, including their homes and jobs
- describe how slaves were treated in the United States

Supporting Your Student

Online Connection *(Mount Vernon)*

For this section, spend some time online with your student and complete the virtual tour of Mount Vernon. You can find websites with lots of helpful visuals and information to help your student understand what life was like for the enslaved individuals under the control of George Washington.

Explore

This lesson can be a sensitive topic. Spend some time answering any questions your student may have while they are reading about slavery and the lives of enslaved people. Here are some tips for handling this subject:

- Teach the era of slavery objectively and from a historical standpoint.
- Don't focus on the physical punishments that slaves received.
- Do not role-play any part of slavery with your student.
- Talk about abolitionists.
- Instead of saying "slaves," use the term "enslaved individuals." This humanizes the enslaved community.

Write *(Describe how slaves were treated in the United States.)*

For this activity, you can assist your student by directing them to the Read "How Enslaved People Were Treated" section. Ask them guiding questions, such as "What did enslaved people eat?," "Why wasn't life fair for enslaved individuals?," and "What weren't enslaved people allowed to do?"

Learning Styles

Auditory learners may enjoy listening to online readings or interviews from formerly enslaved individuals.

Visual learners may enjoy watching a film about the lives of enslaved people. Five kid-approved documentaries about slavery are:

- *Digging for Slaves*
- *Freedom Seekers: Stories from the Western Underground Railroad*
- *Found Voices: The Slave Narratives*
- *Ghosts of Amistad: In the Footsteps of the Rebels*
- *Slavery and the Making of America*

Kinesthetic learners may enjoy touring a plantation or a museum. Search for field trip opportunities within your state to learn more about local places to explore.

Extension Activities

Write a Biography

Help your student to research an enslaved individual and write a biography about that person's life.

Check Out the Library

Take your student on a visit to your local library to search for books about slavery for kids.

Answer Key

Write *(Describe what the homes of enslaved people were like.)*

Answers will vary. Possible answer: Enslaved people lived in small cabins called "slave quarters." These cabins were usually one or two rooms. They were made of wood and often had dirt floors. All of the family members would sleep in the same room.

Write *(Describe how slaves were treated in the United States.)*

Answers will vary. Possible answer: Enslaved people were not treated well. They did not have basic human rights. They didn't have adequate food, clothing, or shelter. Enslaved people were not allowed to learn how to read or write.

Practice

Answers will vary. Possible answers:

House servants: The house servants took care of the house. They cleaned, cooked, did laundry, sewed, and took care of children.

Field hands: Field hands planted and harvested crops, built and repaired structures, and took care of the livestock.

Show What You Know

1. True
2. False
3. False
4. True
5. True
6. True
7. Answers will vary. Possible answer: Frederick Douglass was raised by his grandmother who was a slave. He learned to read and became disobedient toward his masters. Douglass escaped from slavery by disguising himself as a sailor. He became a well-known abolitionist and wrote a famous book about his time as a slave.

Lesson Objectives

By the end of this lesson, your student will be able to:

- identify possible consequences slaves faced when they ran away
- describe the different experiences of runaway slaves
- name Harriet Tubman as an important conductor for the Underground Railroad

Supporting Your Student

Explore

Help your student think of something they are passionate about changing. This could be a local problem—such as the need for more sidewalks in your community—or a global problem—such as overfishing the oceans. Help them create a sign or poster and hang it in a visible space such as on a community mailbox or at the grocery store for other people in your community to see.

Read (Runaway Slaves)

To support your student in this section, emphasize how choosing to escape was a difficult decision for enslaved people to make. You can also point out the language used to describe enslaved people at the time by referencing the wanted posters. Explain to your student how the language has changed over time to show humanity and respect for enslaved individuals.

Write (Describe the experience of a fugitive slave.)

For this activity, encourage your student to look back at the "Read: Runaway Slaves" and "Read: Underground Railroad" sections. Ask your student, "How would it have felt to be a fugitive slave?" Give your student a highlighter to assist them in finding information that they would like to include in this activity.

Learning Styles

Auditory learners may enjoy listening to a book on tape for children about the Underground Railroad or Harriet Tubman's life.

Visual learners may enjoy watching a video for children about the Underground Railroad and the people who helped runaway slaves find freedom.

Kinesthetic learners may enjoy touring a museum to learn more about slavery, the Underground Railroad, abolitionists, the Coffin House, or Harriet Tubman.

Extension Activities

Virtual Tours

Many museums have virtual tours that allow your student to see what life was like for enslaved people without leaving home. Some good resources are found by searching for the following:

- International Museum of Slavery Virtual Tour
- Smithsonian National Museum of African American History & Culture
- Evergreen Plantation Virtual Tour
- Mount Vernon Virtual Tour
- Magnolia Plantation and Gardens – Virtual Tour

Persuasive Letter

Have your student imagine that they are an abolitionist. Have them write a letter to an enslaved person explaining to them why they should escape. This letter should include at least three reasons why they should flee along with information on how to escape, what to bring with them, and where to go.

Answer Key

Write *(What were some of the possible consequences that enslaved people faced if they ran away?)*

Answers will vary. Possible answer: When enslaved people ran away, they could be caught by their owners. If they were caught, they could be sold and separated from their family, beaten, or killed.

Write *(Describe the experience of a fugitive slave.)*

Answers will vary. Possible answers: Fugitive slaves ran away in the middle of the night. They had to be fast and quiet. Fugitive slaves found help through the Underground Railroad, a secret network of people who helped enslaved people to freedom.

Practice

1. True
2. True
3. False
4. True
5. False

Show What You Know

1. C
2. A
3. B
4. D
5. B
6. Answers will vary. Possible answer: The Underground Railroad network assisted hundreds of enslaved people to freedom. Abolitionists hid enslaved people at their homes and gave them a place to sleep and food to eat. If people were caught helping runaway slaves, they were prosecuted by law. If enslaved people were caught during their attempts to run away, they could have been beaten, sold, or killed.

Lesson Objectives

By the end of this lesson, your student will be able to:

- compare Abraham Lincoln's and Stephen Douglas's views about the issue of slavery leading up to the 1860 election
- describe why Kansas had the nickname "Bleeding Kansas"
- recognize that Americans became more divided over the issue of slavery after the Dred Scott case

Supporting Your Student

Explore

Before beginning the reading, prepare your student by discussing slavery in the United States. It is a heavy subject, so be sure to mentally prepare them. Tell them, "Slavery was a part of history. People who experienced enslavement were treated poorly and lost much of their cultural identity." Remind your student that we are learning about real people and they were more than just slaves. They had families, religions, and their own culture. Preparing your student for this subject will help them better understand the material.

Read *(Views on Slavery)*

It would be helpful to create a graphic organizer for your student to fill out during this section. Have three columns: Lincoln's views, Douglas's views, and shared views. This graphic will help your student organize the information as it is presented. Also, it will help them see the similarities and differences in their views.

Write *(What were two causes leading to the Civil War?)*

Have your student reread the sections and highlight phrases about the causes leading to the Civil War. When they do this, they will find two key causes preluding the Civil War. Ask guiding questions like, "Why would the conflict in Kansas lead to a civil war?" Asking questions will help your student think deeper about the worktext.

Learning Styles

Auditory learners may enjoy creating a podcast describing the division over slavery in the United States.

Visual learners may enjoy videos describing the different viewpoints of Douglas and Lincoln over slavery.

Kinesthetic learners may enjoy creating a graphic illustrating the causes of the Civil War and the different views on slavery.

Extension Activities

Read Aloud

Do a read-aloud with your student using a book about slavery. Discuss how slavery impacted the characters and compare the characters' lives with life today. Some book ideas are *Aunt Harriet's Underground Railroad in the Sky* by Faith Ringgold, *BOX: Henry Brown Mails Himself to Freedom* by Carole Boston Weatherford, *Elijah of Buxton* by Christopher Paul Curtis, and *Africa Is My Home: A Child of the Amistad* by Monica Edinger.

Create a News Article

Have your student create a news article summarizing the views on slavery from Lincoln and Douglas. It could be useful to ask them, "What were the main points of difference on ending slavery?" You might also have them draw a picture illustrating the debate between Lincoln and Douglas.

Answer Key

Explore
Answers will vary. Possible answer: Based on this ad, people who were enslaved were viewed as property and not treated with humanity.

Write (What was the difference between Lincoln's and Douglas's views on slavery?)
Answers will vary. Possible answers: Lincoln felt slavery was morally wrong, and the federal government needed to end it. Douglas felt it was up to popular influence to end slavery, not the federal government.

Write (What was the main cause of the conflicts that took place in Kansas?)
Answers will vary. Possible answers: An anti-slavery government being established after the pro-slave laws were passed in Kansas, causing violent warfare.

Write (What were two causes leading to the Civil War?)
Answers will vary. Possible answers: Bleeding Kansas and the Dred Scott case

Show What You Know
1. B
2. A
3. B
4. D
5. B
6. Answers will vary. Possible answers: The Dred Scott case divided the nation over slavery. People who supported slavery celebrated the decision, and anti-slavery people disagreed with the decision. This case further divided the nation over slavery and was one of the many causes of the Civil War.

Lesson Objectives

By the end of this lesson, your student will be able to:

- compare and contrast Northerners', Southerners', and enslaved people's views of slavery
- summarize what the free states thought about slavery

Supporting Your Student

Explore

It would be helpful for your student to create a mind map, with the central circle being "Anti-Slavery Views." Branching off from that circle, make other circles including different views of those against slavery. Creating this graphic will help organize the information and examine the different points of view. These individuals had the same end goal, but different ideas about how to get there.

Read (Views of Slavery)

While reading, it would be helpful to create a chart with three columns: Northerners, Southerners, and enslaved people. In each column, have your student write down different views of people in the United States. This chart will help the student organize the different views people had.

Read (Free States' Views on Slavery)

After reading this section, it would be beneficial to show your student a map of pre-Civil War free states. Point out where the free states tended to be. They were typically in the North, and slave states were in the South. Having the visual of the map will help students see the regional background for the areas' viewpoints on slavery.

Learning Styles

Auditory learners may enjoy listening to a podcast explaining the different points of view on slavery. They may also enjoy listening to sections being read aloud to them.

Visual learners may enjoy looking at maps showing the different regions of the United States and seeing if they were slave states or free states.

Kinesthetic learners may enjoy a scavenger hunt searching for the different points of view on slavery from different leaders and regions. Have pictures of abolitionists such as Fredrick Douglass and leaders of the time with their thoughts on slavery and how they wanted slavery to end or expand.

Extension Activities

Brochure

Have your student create a brochure. On the first panel, have your student add views of slavery from an enslaved person from the North. On the second panel, have them add views of slavery from an enslaved person from the South. Be sure they include images of different leaders during that time.

Create a Video or Podcast

Have your student create a video or podcast summarizing the views the free states had about slavery.

Answer Key

Explore
Answers will vary. Possible answer: Many individuals had different views because they had different experiences. Some people witnessed slavery and others experienced it.

Write *(How did enslaved people view slavery?)*
Answers will vary. Possible answer: Many enslaved people longed for freedom but also feared how they would provide for their needs. Still, they fought for their freedom.

Write *(How did free states view slavery?)*
Answers will vary. Possible answer: People in free states did not want slavery to expand to new territories. They wanted the balance to remain the same between free and slave states.

Practice
Answers will vary. Possible answers:

Northerners: did not want slavery to expand, wanted a balance of political power, did not want the expansion of slavery, worried about jobs if/when enslaved people became free

Southerners: wanted states to decide if they would be a slave state or free state, wanted a balance of political power, worried about jobs if/when enslaved people became free

Enslaved People: wanted freedom and racial justice, did not want the expansion of slavery, worried about jobs if/when enslaved people became free

Show What You Know
1. False
2. True
3. True
4. False
5. True
6. C
7. A
8. Answers will vary. Possible answers: Some abolitionists wanted immediate freedom for all enslaved people. Others wanted the emancipation of enslaved people slowly. Others, including Abraham Lincoln, hoped to keep slavery from expanding.
9. Answers will vary. Possible answers: The North did not want any further expansion of slavery. The South felt the states should decide if they would enter the Union as a free or slave state.
10. Answers will vary. Possible answers: Enslaved people wanted freedom from their harsh working conditions. They feared how they would provide for themselves when they were free.

Lesson Objectives

By the end of this lesson, your student will be able to:

- describe Abraham Lincoln's positions on slavery
- describe how different groups of people felt about the election of Abraham Lincoln as president
- describe how the Democrats were divided in the election of 1860

Supporting Your Student

Explore

When reading this section, have your student highlight key events in Abraham Lincoln's lifetime. When finished, have your student identify the most critical facts for US history. Having these notes will help your student answer the question, "Why was Lincoln important to US history?"

Write (How did Lincoln view slavery and Black people?)

Even though Lincoln wanted slavery to end, it did not mean he saw Black people as equal to white people in society. This question is to check your student's understanding that Lincoln believed every person should have the opportunity to improve the conditions in which they were born. That could not be achieved while enslaved.

Read (Public Opinions of Abraham Lincoln as President)

Before reading this section, it would be helpful to create a graphic organizer. Have three columns: "North," "South," and "Enslaved People." Under each category, have your student write the views they each held about Lincoln's presidency. This graphic will help your student organize the information.

Learning Styles

Auditory learners may enjoy a debate about the pros and cons of Lincoln's presidency. They could do this from a Northerner or abolitionist point of view, explaining why his presidency was good or why it needed improvement.

Visual learners may enjoy creating flashcards to represent all the different views people had on Lincoln's presidency. They could draw the group of people on the front and write their point of view on the back.

Kinesthetic learners may enjoy creating a cause and effect chart about the Democratic Party's split in 1860. They could add drawings to their chart as well.

Extension Activities

Comic Strip

Have your student create a comic strip depicting the cause of the Democratic split in 1860. Have them include dialogue that may have been said between the two sides and pictures showing the two sides debating the issue causing the divide. The comic strip should have at least four squares showing the events.

Poster

Have your student draw or find an image of Abraham Lincoln. Have them write his beliefs about the Union, slavery, and racial equality around the picture.

Answer Key

Online Connection
Your student's research should include Lincoln's:

- Birthday: February 12, 1809
- Birthplace: Larue County, KY
- Presidency: 1861-1865
- Wife: Mary Todd Lincoln
- Three additional facts they found in their research

Explore
Answers will vary. Possible answer: Lincoln was important to US history because he kept the Union together and helped end slavery in the United States.

Write *(How did Lincoln view slavery and Black people?)*
Answers will vary. Possible answer: Lincoln saw slavery as wrong because enslaved people were unable to better their lives and prosper. He did not think they should have the same rights as White people socially or politically.

Write *(What was the criticism about Lincoln's antislavery position from the abolitionists?)*
Answers will vary. Possible answer: Their main criticism was Lincoln was not doing enough politically by not outlining a plan for emancipation.

Practice
Pictures and captions will vary. They should include that Lincoln's main goal was to protect the Union and that he was against slavery.

Show What You Know
1. B
2. A
3. C
4. B
5. False
6. True
7. True

Lesson Objectives

In this lesson, your student will review the following big ideas from Chapter 10.

- The Compromise of 1850 was a series of laws determining if territories acquired in the Mexican-American War would be free states or slave states. (Lesson 56)

- Enslaved people were not treated fairly and did not have fundamental human rights. They often had to work long hours without their needs being adequately met. (Lesson 57)

- The Underground Railroad was a network of people that all worked together to help enslaved people to escape. Enslaved people risked the consequences of capture. (Lesson 58)

- The United States became divided over slavery with different views from leaders. (Lesson 59)

- Northerners, Southerners, and enslaved people had different views about slavery and abolishing it. (Lesson 60)

- Abraham Lincoln was president during a time of divide in the United States over slavery. This divide led to different opinions of Lincoln's presidency. (Lesson 61)

Supporting Your Student

Write (Who were abolitionists?)
Have your student reread the definition and the paragraph about the abolitionists. When your student answers this question, it should be a general answer defining abolitionists in their words. If they would like more of a challenge, they could go through the lesson review or off of their memory and add examples of abolitionists.

Review (Points of View)
Before starting this section, have your student create a mind map. The central circle will be slavery, then off of that circle, have your student add different points of view people had about slavery as they read. This organizer will help them sort the information learned throughout the chapter.

Practice (Vocabulary)
Before starting this activity, review the definitions for each vocabulary word in the word box. Have the student look at each picture. Ask them what vocabulary word each image makes them think about. These questions will help them think of caption ideas in the activity.

Practice (Timeline)
Before drawing the timeline, have your student order the events chronologically. Once the events are in order, double-check that they are correct before the student proceeds. Once they have written down the correct order, have your student write a two-sentence description or picture for each event.

Learning Styles

Auditory learners may enjoy creating a podcast describing the events leading up to the Civil War, such as the Compromise of 1850 and the Dred Scott case. They may also enjoy audiobooks about the experiences of enslaved people using the Underground Railroad.

Visual learners may enjoy cause-and-effect charts, such as how the Compromise of 1850 led to the nation's division and how Bleeding Kansas was a prelude to the Civil War.

Kinesthetic learners may enjoy using sticky notes with the events in this chapter written on them and placing them in the correct order.

Extension Activities

Biography
Have your student research an abolitionist, such as Frederick Douglass, William Lloyd Garrison, Sarah Moore or Angelina Grimké, Harriet Beecher Stowe, or John Brown. Have them write a paper about their life, accomplishments, and view of slavery.

Comic Strip
Have your student create a comic strip depicting one of the events covered in this chapter. Some ideas are the Lincoln and Douglass debate, the Underground Railroad, or the 1860 presidential election.

Answer Key

Write *(Who were abolitionists?)*
Answers will vary. Possible answer: People who wanted slavery to end.

Write *(What was the underground railroad used for?)*
Answers will vary. Possible answer: A network of safe houses for people escaping slavery to use as they made the journey to freedom

Write *(Who supported Lincoln's presidency?)*
Answers will vary. Possible answer: The North and abolitionists supported Lincoln's presidency.

Practice *(Vocabulary)*
Answers will vary. Possible answers:

People of African descent were forced into <u>slavery</u>.

These people are <u>activists</u> for the Earth.

These two people are having a <u>debate</u>.

This is a stamp of Frederick Douglass, a famous <u>abolitionist</u>.

The <u>Emancipation Proclamation</u> freed slaves in the United States.

<u>Congress</u> is where many decisions about the nation are made.

Practice *(Timeline)*
Pictures will vary. Correct order and description of events are:

1. The Compromise of 1850: The US Congress passed laws about the new territory gained after the Mexican-American War. To make the North happy, Congress ended the slave trade and California entered the Union as a free state. To make the South happy, the territories of New Mexico and Utah were open to slavery.

2. Bleeding Kansas: In Kansas, people who were anti-slavery became upset over the pro-slavery legislation being passed. This led to people who were anti-slavery starting their own government and led to violent disputes, which were a prelude to the Civil War.

3. Dred Scott case: Dred Scott vs. Sandford in 1857 was an important decision of the US Supreme Court. The Court maintained that the Constitution did not intend to include American citizenship for people of African descent.

4. The Democratic Party divide: In 1860, the Democratic Party became divided when they could not decide on a candidate for president. They ended up splitting and having two candidates: the Southern, pro-slavery candidate and the Northern, anti-slavery candidate.

5. The results of the 1860 presidential election: The presidential election named Abraham Lincoln as the 16th president. The North and abolitionists supported it, and the South did not, which led to them seceding from the Union.

Practice *(Points of View Graphic Organizer)*
Answers will vary. Possible answer:

The North	The South	Enslaved People	Abraham Lincoln
The North did not want slavery to expand. Their goal was not to end slavery.	The South saw slavery as needed since they did rely on enslaved people's labor on plantations.	People who were enslaved saw slavery as inhumane and morally wrong. They wanted freedom and racial justice.	Abraham Lincoln saw slavery as morally wrong, but he did not know how to end it within the Constitution's restraints or political system.

Quick Review

Refer to the statement your student circled in the Show What You Know section to self-assess their knowledge of the chapter concepts. Then to assist in determining if your student is ready to take the assessment, consider:

- Having your student identify the different points of view on slavery.
- Having your student state the causes leading to a division in the United States.
- Having your student describe the living conditions enslaved people had to endure
- Having your student indicate the different opinions about Abraham Lincoln's presidency.

Chapter Assessment

Match each vocabulary word to its definition.

1. ____ compromise

2. ____ Congress

3. ____ debate

4. ____ dispute

5. ____ abolitionist

6. ____ Juneteenth

7. ____ slavery

8. ____ Underground Railroad

9. ____ activism

10. ____ emancipation

A. freeing a person from slavery

B. one who works to end the practice of slavery

C. a network of people who offered shelter and assistance to escaping enslaved people

D. the celebration of the end of slavery in the United States

E. the practice of people owning other people

F. a group of representatives from different colonies or states that make decisions for the whole country

G. a disagreement, argument, or debate

H. a structured argument where both sides try to prove that they are correct

I. an agreement to a dispute where both sides agree on the solution

J. action to make a change within society

Choose the correct answer for each question.

11. Who was Harriet Tubman? Circle all correct answers.

   A. a formerly enslaved person

   B. a conductor on the Underground Railroad

   C. a nurse during the Civil War

   D. a spy for the North during the Civil War

12. What was the Dred Scott decision?

   A. slavery was unconstitutional

   B. free African Americans had Constitutional rights

   C. the Constitution did not intend to include American citizenship for people of African descent

   D. slavery could expand in new territories gained

Discover! SOCIAL STUDIES • GRADE 4 • CHAPTER 10 ASSESSMENT

185

13. What was the Underground Railroad?

    A. a train that took people between the North and the South

    B. a train system that used underground tunnels

    C. a network of people and safe houses that assisted enslaved people in their journey to freedom

    D. network of people who returned enslaved people back to their owners

14. How did most Northerners view slavery?

    A. they did not want the expansion of slavery

    B. they wanted slavery to end in all of the US

    C. they wanted slavery to expand

    D. they were abolitionists

Answer the following questions in complete sentences.

15. Describe how the Underground Railroad assisted people escaping slavery and the possible consequences for both the person seeking freedom and the people who helped them.

....

....

....

16. How did abolitionist views differ from Abraham Lincoln's view of slavery?

....

....

....

17. Describe the lives of people who experienced slavery.

....

....

....

Chapter Assessment Answer Key

1. I
2. F
3. H
4. G
5. B
6. D
7. E
8. C
9. J
10. A
11. A, B, C, D
12. C
13. C
14. A
15. Answers will vary. Possible answers: The Underground Railroad assisted hundreds of enslaved people to freedom. Abolitionists hid enslaved people at their homes and gave them a place to sleep and food to eat. If people were caught helping runaway slaves, they were prosecuted by law. If enslaved people got caught during their attempts to run away, they could have been beaten, sold, or killed.
16. Answers will vary. Possible answers: Lincoln and abolitionists both saw slavery as morally wrong. Lincoln's first goal was keeping the Union together and did not know how to end slavery within the political system. Abolitionists knew slavery had to end despite the political system.
17. Answers will vary. Possible answers: Enslaved people barely had their basic needs met and worked long hours. Some worked in the fields, and others worked as servants. They were often sold and separated from their families and communities.

Discover! SOCIAL STUDIES • GRADE 4 • CHAPTER 10 ASSESSMENT

187

Alternative Assessment

Project: Historical Fiction

Historical fiction is a piece of fictional literature that is based on or around a historical time period or event.

Project Requirements or Steps:

For this project, write a short piece of historical fiction based on an event or period in history from the chapter. You will exercise your research skills and work to convey a historical event or time period as realistically as possible.

Include the following elements:

1. Title related to the chapter
2. Reference to an important event or period in history on which the writing will be based
3. Plot progression or a clear storyline
4. Well-developed characters
5. Literary elements, such as figurative language
6. Connection to the chapter through setting, characters, plot, etc.

188

Discover! SOCIAL STUDIES • GRADE 4 • CHAPTER 10 ASSESSMENT

Alternative Assessment Rubric

Use the following rubric to grade your student's assessment.

	4	3	2	1	Points
Accuracy and Relevance	The work has many characteristics or examples that tie it to an historical event or time period. The connections to history are academically advanced and indicate a great deal of effort.	The work has several characteristics or examples that tie it to an historical event or time period.	The work has one or two characteristics or examples that tie it to an historical event or time period.	The work has no connections to history.	
Quality	The work exceeds expectations. The storyline is very interesting and high quality.	The work is of good quality, but there is some room for improvement.	The work has many areas that could be improved.	The work is very low quality.	
Creativity	The work is creative and original and very interesting to the reader.	The work is somewhat creative and original and interesting to the reader.	The work is not very creative or original, but it is interesting to the reader.	The work is not creative or interesting.	
Grammar and Mechanics	The work has no grammar or punctuation issues and uses advanced vocabulary.	The work contains a few grammar or punctuation mistakes and age-appropriate vocabulary.	The work contains several grammar and punctuation mistakes and age-appropriate vocabulary.	The work contains a distracting number of grammar and punctuation mistakes and overly-simplified vocabulary.	

Total Points _____/16

Average _____

Discover! SOCIAL STUDIES • GRADE 4 • CHAPTER 10 ASSESSMENT

189

The Confederate States of America

Lesson Objectives

By the end of this lesson, your student will be able to:

- identify the seven states that first joined together to form the Confederate States of America
- describe how West Virginia became its own state

Supporting Your Student

Explore
Deepen your student's understanding of this topic by going on a drive on a highway and discussing the questions posed. You can ask your student guiding questions like, "What would it be like if one person was driving the wrong way down the highway?," "What if it were a whole group of people?," and "How would that be different?"

Take a Closer Look (Abraham Lincoln)
Encourage your student to review the lesson "Abraham Lincoln" to help activate their prior knowledge about the election of 1860. This will prepare them to answer the questions more fully.

Read (West Virginia)
To help your student see how eastern Virginians were using their power, you can ask guiding questions like, "How can wealth contribute to power?," "How did eastern Virginians use this power?," and "How did they make the system work better for enslavers than non-enslavers?"

Learning Styles

Auditory learners may enjoy doing a choral reading with you in certain sections of the reading, like the first paragraph of each Read section.

Visual learners may enjoy labeling their own map of Confederate and Union states in 1861, as well as the territories.

Kinesthetic learners may enjoy completing the Practice activity using whole-body movement. On a sidewalk or driveway, write Union and Confederacy on the ground with a line between them. Read the options to your student, and they can jump to the correct side to indicate their answer.

Extension Activities

A Virginian's Lament
Have your student imagine that they are a western Virginian wanting change in the state government. They should write a letter to someone out of state explaining the troubles in Virginia and how they are affected by them.

Sorting States
Write the name of each state in 1861 on separate slips of paper. Have your student draw them out of a container, one at a time. They should sort each slip into two piles: Union and Confederacy.

Answer Key

Write *(Why did the Confederate states want to secede before Lincoln took office?)*
Answers will vary. Possible answer: The original Confederate states seceded because they were afraid Lincoln's election meant that slavery would be prohibited from expanding into the Western Territories.

Write *(Based on the similarities and differences between constitutions, what were the major priorities of the Confederate States of America?)*
Answers will vary. Possible answer: Confederate priorities included protecting slavery, limiting the ways the government could raise and spend money, controlling currency, and limiting states' ability to make treaties with each other.

Practice
1. Confederacy
2. Union
3. Union
4. Confederacy
5. Union

Show What You Know
1. Louisiana
2. Florida
3. Texas
4. South Carolina
5. Alabama
6. Mississippi
7. Georgia
8. Answers will vary. Possible answer: Tensions between eastern and western Virginians grew over disagreements about government. Western Virginians wanted more democratically elected officials and more of a voice in politics. After Virginia voted to secede from the Union, a group in the west held a convention to vote on forming a separate state from Virginia. A state constitution was drafted and revised to meet all requirements to establish a new state, and West Virginia was admitted to the Union.

Lesson Objectives

By the end of this lesson, your student will be able to:

- identify states that became a part of the Confederate States of America after the Battle of Fort Sumter
- summarize the main causes of the Battle of Fort Sumter
- identify the main events that occurred during the Battle of Fort Sumter

Supporting Your Student

Explore

This section is an excellent teaching moment to discuss the importance of standing up for important beliefs, but also having discernment to know when it's time to stop and hear the other side out. You can extend this conversation by role-playing or discussing made-up scenarios to give your student a chance to imagine what they might do in those moments.

Read (Tensions Increase)

The Civil War-era defense strategy is likely not extremely familiar to your student. Help them imagine the realities of defending Fort Moultrie by closely examining the aerial photo. Point out that the position of guns and cannons was facing outward toward the water. Ask, "Why would that be?" or "Why wouldn't they have arms aimed in the other direction?" Remind them that since South Carolina is on the East Coast, an attack from behind on land was improbable as another country would be coming by sea. Point out the walls and discuss sand dunes and the possibility of climbing over the walls easier with the piled-up sand.

Read (The Point of No Return)

Ask your student what they think of President Buchanan's idea to send an unarmed merchant ship with supplies instead of a naval ship. Remind them of the interaction between President Buchanan and Governor Pickens. Ask your student extension questions like, "How do you think their miscommunication affected how South Carolina responded to seeing the *Star of the West* in the harbor?" and "Did President Buchanan have any better options? Did Governor Pickens?"

Learning Styles

Auditory learners may enjoy listening to narratives of accounts from the Fort Sumter conflict.

Visual learners may enjoy examining maps of the South Carolina coast to imagine alternative strategies the United States could have used to defend federal buildings or resupply Major Anderson's troops.

Kinesthetic learners may enjoy answering question one for the Show What You Know section by playing "Up or Down" instead of circling. Say the state options aloud for your student, and have them jump up on the four states that seceded immediately following Fort Sumter.

Extension Activities

Virtual Field Trip

Your student can view a virtual field trip of Fort Sumter online. Have your student write a paragraph after viewing that explains how their understanding or perspective changed after watching it.

Comparing Reports

Have your student view news articles reporting the Battle of Fort Sumter. A collection is available through the Library of Congress. Your student can compare and contrast the way the news is reported in Confederate states, Union states, and border states. After they compare the reports, ask your student this reflection question: "How would the tone and approach of the news articles influence the opinions of people in each state?"

Answer Key

Write *(Why was Fort Sumter a better strategic position for the US Army?)*

Answers will vary. Possible answer: Fort Sumter was surrounded by water, so an attacking force could not approach on foot like they could with Fort Moultrie. Fort Sumter was built to be a much stronger fort, with better defenses than Fort Moultrie.

Practice

1. B
2. D
3. A
4. C

Show What You Know

1. Virginia, Tennessee, Arkansas, North Carolina
2. True
3. Answers will vary. Possible answer: One major cause for the Battle of Fort Sumter was the Secretary of War's decision to tell Major Anderson that he could move if he needed to without consulting the President. Because the President knew about this approval, he said things that later made Governor Pickens feel lied to. It was a very serious situation, and communication should have been clear between everyone. This misunderstanding made South Carolina less likely to trust or work with the US government. If the Secretary of War had talked to the President first, tensions may not have risen as much.

Lesson Objectives

By the end of this lesson, your student will be able to:

- compare and contrast the strengths and weaknesses of the North and the South
- compare the positions of General Robert E. Lee and General Winfield Scott on the war

Supporting Your Student

Explore

It can be challenging for your student to imagine going to war against their own neighbors or siblings. To help your student better understand this context, ask them who they would least like to face in a war. Ask how it would make them feel to fight against that person. Ask them if they would be able to keep duty and their feelings for that person separate, like James and Alexander Campbell, were able to.

Read (General Winfield Scott)

It might be difficult for your student to understand why Scott wanted to use the Anaconda Plan or why the media criticized it for being too passive. Ask your student guided questions, such as, "Why do you think the newspapers and other people wanted the Union Army to act more aggressively?" and "Why do you think General Scott didn't like that idea?"

Read (General Robert E. Lee)

Your student may have some familiarity or recognition of the name Robert E. Lee, but might have some misconceptions about him. It is important for your student to make the distinction between relying on brigadier generals and having command organized under a single major general. Reiterate that Lee did not have command of the Confederate Army at the start of the war and was not responsible for the South's initial war strategy.

Read (Advantages and Disadvantages)

Help your student make connections to the advantages and disadvantages listed by asking guided questions like, "It says gunpowder was an import, and the navy could block imports to the South. Do you think this is why blockading southern ports was an important strategy?" and "Southern states did have enslaved people they could force to fight, but do you think that always worked out as they planned? Would enslaved people want to fight to keep themselves enslaved?"

Learning Styles

Auditory learners may enjoy listening to a podcast about Civil War strategy.

Visual learners may enjoy looking at battle and strategy maps of the Civil War to see how these ideas translated to reality.

Kinesthetic learners may enjoy completing the T-chart on poster board or chart paper by writing their advantages on sticky notes and attaching them on either side.

Extension Activities

Women of the Civil War

Your student may be curious about the contributions of women during the Civil War. There were many! They can research how women contributed to the war effort and find out more about notable women during this time. Have your student make a poster about one notable woman and her achievements/contributions.

War Strategy Checkers

Play a game of checkers with your student, allowing them to select which type of strategy they would prefer to use: Scott's Anaconda Plan of blocking and slowly choking out the competition or Lee's risky and aggressive strategy.

Answer Key

Write *(Scott chose the Union despite his Virginia roots, and Lee had his pick of command posts in either Army. How does this support and relate to the idea that the Civil War was fought "brother against brother"?)*
Answers will vary. Possible answer: Both Scott and Lee could have fought against their own neighbors or relatives.

Practice

Answers will vary. Possible answers: northern strategy—Anaconda Plan, organized under a major general, more established and unified army, using a brigadier general in battle because Scott was too old; southern strategy—state militias working alongside Confederate Army, no central major general with full command of the military, no singular strategy, had to form army after the new government was established; similarities—disagreements with presidents on both sides, both sides wanted to recruit Robert E. Lee, almost equal number of troops (in the beginning)

Show What You Know

1. Answers will vary. Possible answers:
   Northern Advantages: older and more established government and military, control of manufacturing and transportation, larger population, diplomatic relationships with other countries
   Southern Advantages: morale and the energy of defending their own home and way of life, fighting mostly on their own land, enslaved people they could force to fight, control of food production, determination/resourcefulness

2. Answers will vary. Possible answer: Winfield Scott had the better strategy at the start of the war because he had a single plan. That plan would get them through the entire war instead of thinking about things battle-by-battle. Even though it wasn't as aggressive as others might have wanted, it gave the army an overall plan. When they attacked too soon with Irving McDowell, they lost. Following a single plan makes

the most of the strengths the North had, like an established military.

Lesson Objectives

By the end of this lesson, your student will be able to:

- identify important Civil War leaders from the North and South
- identify and analyze how early battles and events affected the war

Supporting Your Student

Explore

Your student isn't expected to know the answers to these statements. Instead, discuss whether each statement could be accurate with your student based on their prior knowledge of the Civil War. You may want to discuss what your student already knows about the Civil War before reading and discussing the statements.

Read (Leaders of the Civil War)

You may want to describe the end of the last battle when the Confederates surrendered at Appomattox Court House. You may want to explain that at this point, the South knew they couldn't win.

Write (Describe what happened during these battles in your own words.)

Before writing their summary, have your student take notes about each battle. That will make it easier for them to write their summary about the battles.

Practice

If your student is struggling with the practice activity, have them reread the texts and discuss those texts with them. You and your student could take notes together about each person or battle.

Learning Styles

Auditory learners may enjoy listening to an audio story or audiobook about the Civil War. There are several kids' books on book websites.

Visual learners may enjoy watching a documentary about the leaders and battles of the Civil War. They can discuss what they learned about the Civil War.

Kinesthetic learners may enjoy creating a timeline of the main events of the Civil War, especially about the battles.

Extension Activities

Memory Game

To better memorize the information about the leaders of the Civil War, play a memory game. Have your student write the name of each leader on an index card, and a description of each leader on an index card. Shuffle them and place them face down. Play a game of memory by matching cards with your student.

Battle Statistics Graph

Have your student research each battle. Have them find out the number of casualties and wounded for each side. Have your student create a graph about the battle statistics.

Answer Key

Explore

The following statements are true:

One leader left his strategy plans behind, and they were picked up by the other side.

Robert E. Lee and Stonewall Jackson fought for the Confederacy.

The Civil War began at Fort Sumter in South Carolina.

Write (Who do you think led the Union to victory?)

Answers will vary. Possible answer: Ulysses S. Grant is responsible for leading the Union to victory. He took over when the last general was having trouble and led the troops to victory.

Write (Describe what happened during these battles in your own words.)

Answers will vary. Possible answer: At the Battle of Antietam, Robert E. Lee had left his plans behind, so the Union Army found them and used them. At the Battle of Gettysburg, the Confederates struggled to push the Union Army back. They tried at Pickett's Charge, but lost. At the Siege of Vicksburg, the Union Army starved the Confederates by stopping their supplies from coming in.

Practice

1. B
2. G
3. C
4. E
5. A
6. D
7. F

Show What You Know

1. appointed
2. J.E.B. Stuart
3. Fort Sumter
4. Vicksburg
5. Robert E. Lee
6. Jefferson Davis
7. Antietam
8. Stonewall Jackson
9. Gettysburg
10. George McClellan

Lesson Objectives

By the end of this lesson, your student will be able to:

- identify that the Emancipation Proclamation granted freedom to slaves in the Confederacy
- describe how the Emancipation Proclamation impacted the United States
- identify ways Black regiments of soldiers contributed to the war
- recognize that slavery was made illegal in all states by the Thirteenth Amendment

Supporting Your Student

Explore

If your student is struggling with determining which states fought for the North and which fought for the South, you may want to provide the border states (i.e., Delaware, West Virginia, Missouri, Kentucky, and Maryland).

Read (What Is the Emancipation Proclamation?)

Discuss the Emancipation Proclamation with your student, especially how it only freed slaves in the Confederate states. Your student may wonder why the Union states were not included in this document. Lincoln created the Emancipation Proclamation as a military strategy during the war. The border states were also not included because he did not want them to get angry and join the Confederacy.

Write (What did the Emancipation Proclamation do?)

If your student doesn't know what to write for this question, you may want to discuss what was read in the text about the Emancipation Proclamation. Encourage your student to take notes while they are reading the text.

Practice

You may want to review the vocabulary words and their meanings prior to your student completing this vocabulary activity.

Learning Styles

Auditory learners may enjoy listening to a historian describe facts about the Emancipation Proclamation, the 54th Massachusetts Infantry, and the Thirteenth Amendment.

Visual learners may enjoy visiting a museum about the Civil War and the Emancipation Proclamation.

Kinesthetic learners may enjoy creating a three-dimensional timeline with supplies relating to the Emancipation Proclamation and other events from this lesson.

Extension Activities

Comic Proclamation

Have your student create a comic strip of the main events of the Emancipation Proclamation. First, have them write down five to eight events that occurred with the Emancipation Proclamation. Then have them draw each event and write the event under it. Your student may want to color their comic strip.

Photo Analysis

Find photos of the 54th Massachusetts Infantry and other photos or pictures of Black regiments. Discuss with your student what they see in those pictures. How do you think these military regiments differed from others?

198

Disc*ver! SOCIAL STUDIES • GRADE 4 • LESSON 67

Answer Key

Explore

The southern Confederate states that should be shaded gray are North Carolina, Virginia, South Carolina, Florida, Georgia, Alabama, Mississippi, Tennessee, Louisiana, Arkansas, and Texas.

The northern Union states that should be shaded blue are Oregon, Nevada, California, Iowa, Minnesota, Wisconsin, Michigan, Kansas, Illinois, Indiana, Ohio, New Jersey, Pennsylvania, Rhode Island, Connecticut, Massachusetts, Vermont, New Hampshire, New York, and Maine.

The border states that should be shaded green are Kentucky, Missouri, Maryland, Delaware, and West Virginia.

Write (What did the Emancipation Proclamation do?)

Answers will vary. Possible answer: The Emancipation Proclamation declared that the slaves in the southern Confederate states were freed.

Write (How did the Black regiments contribute to the Civil War?)

Answers will vary. Possible answer: The Black regiments contributed to the Civil War by fighting in several battles, including the Second Battle of Fort Wagner.

Practice

Answers will vary. Possible answer:

1. Children are prohibited from driving a car.
2. Soldiers are the people in a military regiment.
3. If a document is ratified, it means that everyone has agreed.
4. My mom can prohibit me from eating sweets before dinner.
5. A regiment would fight in a war.

Show What You Know

1. False
2. False
3. True
4. True
5. True
6. False
7. True
8. False

Lesson Objectives

By the end of this lesson, your student will be able to:

- describe the improvements and advancements of weaponry during the Civil War
- describe how railroads and telegraphs were used during the Civil War

Supporting Your Student

Explore

Your student may need some help in getting started with this activity. One way to help would be to look up the weapons used during the Revolutionary War or the War of 1812.

Write *(Which improvement do you think was most helpful to the Civil War?)*

Discuss each improvement with your student. Your student may even want to look up more information about each improvement.

Read *(Civil War Weapons)*

You may want to show other pictures of the weapons so that your student can better understand what the weapon looks like. Then discuss how the weapon works and how it would benefit the soldiers during the Civil War.

Practice

To help your student, have them focus on the vocabulary words in the text. Review those words before doing this practice activity.

Learning Styles

Auditory learners may enjoy listening to a Civil War podcast about the weapons and improvements in the Civil War.

Visual learners may enjoy creating a collage of pictures of weapons, ships, and technological advancements. Find pictures online or draw them. Then glue them to a piece of paper.

Kinesthetic learners may enjoy creating a small-scale model of one of the technological advancements using craft and art supplies.

Extension Activities

Diorama

Have your student create a diorama of a scene of a Civil War battle, including the weapons and advancements. Your student will use a shoebox and create their scene with pictures, arts, and craft supplies.

Civil War Reenactment

Have your student attend a Civil War reenactment to see the types of weapons they used during the Civil War.

Answer Key

Explore
Answers will vary. Possible answer: a rifle with a bayonet, submarines, hot air balloons, Gatling gun

Write *(Which improvement do you think was most helpful to the Civil War?)*
Answers will vary. Possible answer: The most helpful improvement to the Civil War would be the Army Ambulance Corps because the soldiers had a better chance of survival.

Write *(How was the rifled musket slower compared to the Gatling gun?)*
Answers will vary. Possible answer: The rifled musket was much slower than the Gatling gun because the Gatling gun could shoot rounds much faster at 400 rounds per minute. The rifled musket had to be loaded by the soldier for each round.

Practice
1. D
2. B
3. A
4. E
5. C

Show What You Know
1. E
2. B
3. H
4. D
5. G
6. F
7. A
8. C

Lesson Objectives

By the end of this lesson, your student will be able to:

- recognize the history of the American Red Cross and how the organization helps during times of war
- explain the importance of the Battle of Gettysburg and the Battle of Vicksburg
- evaluate a wartime strategy, such as General Sherman's March to the Sea

Supporting Your Student

Read (The American Red Cross)

To help your student better understand the objectives of the American Red Cross, it may be helpful for your student to learn the organization's origins as influenced by Clara Barton's trip to Europe. To do this, have your student research videos on the International Red Cross by using an online search engine. Your student may notice some key similarities between the International Red Cross and American Red Cross, including its mission to help people in times of war and natural disasters. Discuss with them how the American Red Cross provided relief to soldiers during notable American wars and how the organization helps victims of natural disasters today.

Read (The Battles of Vicksburg and Gettysburg)

As your student reads through this section in the worktext, it may be helpful to retrieve additional American Civil War maps by using an online search engine. Reinforce your student's understanding of Union and Confederate states by asking them to point out the locations of America's once divided nation. As your student reads about the Battle of Vicksburg, have them locate the Mississippi River and assess the states in which it crosses on the map. Help your student understand the importance of the Union's capture of this river by pointing out that it is the main transportation route between the North and the South. Similarly, as your student reads about the Battle of Gettysburg, have them locate Gettysburg, Pennsylvania, which was part of the Union. Ask your student how the Civil War may have turned out if the Confederates claimed Gettysburg.

Practice

Help your student complete the table by encouraging them to focus on one column at a time. Start by going over the first column, which includes the key events and organizations of the Civil War. In the second column, have your student evaluate the key features of each event and organization. In the third column, have your student brainstorm the impacts these key events and organizations had on society.

Learning Styles

Auditory learners may enjoy listening to a podcast on the Civil War.

Visual learners may enjoy creating a Civil War flip-book that features key figures, such as Abraham Lincoln, Clara Barton, William Tecumseh Sherman, Robert E. Lee, and Harriet Tubman. They may also include key events, such as the Battles of Vicksburg and Gettysburg, General Sherman's March to the Sea, the Underground Railroad, and the Emancipation Proclamation.

Kinesthetic learners may enjoy learning about basic first aid by preparing a first aid kit that includes bandages, sterile gauze, a pair of scissors, tweezers, antibiotic ointment, alcohol wipes, a cold compress, examination gloves, adhesive tape, and cotton buds. Research and review how to handle injuries such as minor burns, a twisted ankle, or a bloody nose.

Extension Activities

Natural Disaster Preparation

Have your student search "The Pillowcase Project", which is an activity created by the American Red Cross, by using an online search engine. Here your student will learn how to prepare for different emergencies, such as hurricanes, earthquakes, wildfires, and winter storms. Have your student read what each emergency is and review safety tips by performing a series of activities from dragging and dropping words to answering questions. Discuss each of these emergencies in detail to reinforce important prevention strategies with your student.

Civil War Heroes on a Cereal Box

Have your students create a breakfast cereal box in memory of an important Civil War figure. Have your student use an actual (preferably empty) cereal box that they can apply paper to. Your student may use a mailing cardboard box as an alternative. Then have your student cover up the box with different images that pertain to their chosen Civil War figure (i.e., important battles) by using an online search engine or by drawing.

On the sides of the box where one normally finds the nutritional information, ask your student to craft a timeline of key events in this historical figure's life. Encourage creativity by asking your student to create a game, such as a crossword puzzle or word search that relates to the Civil War, on the back of the box. Finally, ask your student to create a name for the cereal!

Answer Key

Explore

Answers will vary. Possible answers: The American Red Cross provides food, water, and shelter to people during natural disasters. They may also provide medication and disaster relief, such as building new houses or donating money to different organizations.

Write (What kind of assistance did the American Red Cross provide during wars?)

Answers will vary. Possible answers: During wars, the American Red Cross provided medical care to soldiers, created hospital ships and trains, recruited nurses, sent supplies to American soldiers, and created the first national blood donation program.

Write (What was the importance of the Battles of Vicksburg and Gettysburg?)

Answers will vary. Possible answers: In the Battle of Vicksburg, the Union captured the Mississippi River, which was the last port controlled by the Confederates. This weakened the Confederacy. The Battle of Gettysburg was a turning point and the deadliest battle in the Civil War. Union soldiers outnumbered Confederate soldiers, which led to more weakening of the Confederacy. Over time it also led to the Union victory of the Civil War and the end of slavery.

Write (What was General Sherman's wartime strategy and why was it successful?)

Answers will vary. Possible answers: The new strategy was called total war, and it was used to prevent Confederate soldiers and civilians from creating militaries. Sherman's army burned down Confederate businesses, civilian homes, and military supplies. This strategy was very successful because it not only targeted soldiers but also civilians.

Practice

Answers will vary. Possible answers:

Key Events and Organizations	Features	Impact on Society
American Red Cross	They provide humanitarian aid (such as food, water, shelter, clothing, and blood donation) and disaster-prevention training, such as first aid.	It protects human life and health in times of crisis.
Battle of Vicksburg	The Union states captured and controlled the Mississippi River.	The Confederates were cut off from receiving war supplies to aid their growing army; Some Confederate states became isolated; This led to Union victory and the end of slavery.
Battle of Gettysburg	This battle only lasted for three days but was the deadliest battle in the Civil War; Union soldiers outnumbered Confederate soldiers.	It ultimately led to Union victory and the end of slavery.
General Sherman's March	Sherman's March to the Sea was about 285 miles long; It stretched from Atlanta to the Confederate coastal town of Savannah; His new strategy was called total war and was used to prevent Confederate soldiers and civilians from creating militaries; Sherman's army burned down Confederate businesses and civilian houses.	It significantly weakened the power and economy of the Confederates. This ultimately led to Union victory.

Show What You Know

1. True
2. False
3. False
4. A, B, C
5. A, C
6. D
7. B

Lesson Objectives

By the end of this lesson, your student will be able to:

- identify the main events that resulted in General Lee surrendering his forces
- describe the main points of Lincoln's plan to bring peace to the North and South
- identify the effects that the assassination of Lincoln had on the country

Supporting Your Student

Read (Uniting of the North and South)

To help your student better understand the Reconstruction era, it may be helpful to search for photos or videos that show the extent of the property, life, and crop devastation in the Confederate states by using an online search engine. Discuss with your student President Lincoln's plans for Reconstruction and how he developed them. For example, President Lincoln wanted to be lenient with his punishment to the South because his main goal was to reunite the divided country as one nation. He planned to issue pardons for any Southerner who took an oath to be faithful to the Union. Although he was never able to implement his plans due to his assassination, ask your student the following questions: "Were President Lincoln's plans for Reconstruction fair? Why or why not?"

Read (Effects of Lincoln's Assassination)

As your student reads through this section in the worktext, it may be helpful for them to search for videos or articles that describe the events leading up to President Lincoln's assassination. Understanding the cause of his death is key to understanding the tense conditions that continued to prevail in the United States even after the Emancipation Proclamation and Lincoln's goals of unity. It may also benefit your student to review the laws created in the Black Codes for African Americans, so they can better understand the implications restricted freedoms had on their way of life. To do this, encourage your student to look for photos depicting people abiding by Black Code laws, including separate restrooms and water fountains for Whites and African Americans.

Practice

Help your student complete the table by encouraging them to focus on one column at a time. Start by going over the first column, which includes the key events and organizations of the Civil War. In the second column, have your student evaluate the key features of each event and organization. In the third column, have your student brainstorm the impacts these key events and organizations had on society.

Learning Styles

Auditory learners may enjoy recording a podcast to introduce and describe famous events during the Civil War—such as the Gettysburg Address and President Lincoln's assassination—and after the Civil War—including the Reconstruction era, the Thirteenth, Fourteenth, and Fifteenth Amendements, and Black Codes.

Visual learners may enjoy creating a Civil War crossword puzzle using key terms, such as the Union, Confederates, President Lincoln, General Lee, Reconstruction, Black codes, North, South, Gettysburg Address, and slavery.

Kinesthetic learners may enjoy making popular food recipes from the Civil War era, including gingersnap cookies, cucumber tea sandwiches, fresh-mulled cider, and mince pie.

Extension Activities

Civil War Storybook

Have your student research what it was like being a kid during the Civil War by using an online search engine. Ask your student to investigate the differences in the way of life for kids from the North and South during the nineteenth century. Encourage your student to write a story with illustrations that details the way of life, triumphs, and challenges those kids went through. For example, life for kids across the North and the South was hard during the Civil War. Many children parted with their fathers, brothers, and uncles, as they enlisted in the war, or joined the military themselves. In fact, as many as 20 percent of Civil War soldiers were younger than 18. That was the minimum recruiting age for Union soldiers, but many people willingly overlooked the law. The Confederacy set no minimum age. By comparison, children in the South, particularly slaves, were often overworked, succumbed to illnesses, or were prevented from receiving an education.

Lights, Cameras, Reconstruction!

Have your student perform a skit of an important event during the Reconstruction era, such as the creation of the Black Codes, the ratification of the Thirteenth, Fourteenth, and Fifteenth Amendments, the Compromise of 1877, the formation of Freedmen's Bureau, and the creation of the Ku Klux Klan. As your student performs their skit, encourage them to think about the impacts (whether positive or negative) their particular reenactment had on American society. Keep in mind that some of these topics may be sensitive for your student, so it is encouraged that instructors teach these subjects as objectively as possible. To do this, approach these topics from a historical standpoint and encourage your student to ask questions. For more information about teaching race and slavery in the United States, visit learningforjustice.org.

Answer Key

Explore

Answers will vary. Possible answers: The Gettysburg Address stressed the unity and equality of people under one nation. It also encouraged people to help America's democracy, fought for the rights of African Americans, and honored the soldiers who died in the Civil War.

Write (Name and describe two reasons that General Lee surrendered to the Union.)

Answers will vary. Possible answers: The Confederates were low on troops and supplies, and some of the troops deserted their war zones.

Write (Describe President Lincoln's plan for reuniting the North and South.)

Answers will vary. Possible answers: President Abraham Lincoln wanted to be lenient to the South. He proposed the following Reconstruction plans: any Southerner who took an oath to the Union would be given a pardon. He also stated that if 10 percent of Confederate voters supported the Union, including making slavery illegal, then that state could be readmitted.

Write (How did Lincoln's assassination affect society?)

Answers will vary. Possible answers: The implementation of President Andrew Johnson's Reconstruction plans, the creation of the Black codes, the ratification of the Thirteenth, Fourteenth, and Fifteenth Amendments, the fight for racial equality among African Americans.

Learning Styles

Auditory learners may enjoy listening to a podcast on the Civil War, President Abraham Lincoln, or the Reconstruction era. They may enjoy listening to these famous historical figures and events through *Kids Listen* or *The Civil War* podcasts.

Visual learners may enjoy visiting a Civil War museum or monument virtually or in person. Notable Civil War museums include the National Civil War Museum (Harrisburg, Pennsylvania), the American Civil War Museum (Richmond, Virginia), and the National Museum of Civil War Medicine (Frederick, Maryland). Famous monuments include the Fort Sumter National Monument (Charleston, South Carolina), the Shiloh National Military Park (Shiloh, Tennessee), the Vicksburg National Military Park (Vicksburg, Mississippi), and the Gettysburg National Military Park (Gettysburg, Pennsylvania).

Kinesthetic learners may enjoy learning about basic first aid by preparing a first-aid kit that includes bandages, sterile gauzes, a pair of scissors, tweezers, antibiotic ointment, alcohol wipes, cold compress, examination gloves, adhesive tape rolls, and/or cotton buds. Research and review how to handle injuries, such as minor burns, cuts and scrapes, a twisted ankle, or a bloody nose.

Extension Activities

Letter to President Lincoln
Have your student pretend that they have been transported back to the year 1865 to warn President Lincoln of his assassination. However, they have been informed that they must not reveal themselves to Lincoln or civilians that they are from the future. To interact with Lincoln, they can only write a letter to him. Have your student write a letter to Lincoln warning him of the events that will unfold on the night of his assassination. Encourage your student to introduce themselves in the letter, include details of the impending assassination, the culprit's name, and prevention strategies for Lincoln. For example, your student may suggest that Lincoln avoid going to the Ford Theatre on the evening of April 14, 1865 or to have police officers investigate John Wilkes Booth and his co-conspirators.

Civil War Heroes on a Cereal Box
Have your student create a breakfast cereal box in memory of an important Civil War figure discussed in or outside the worktext. Your student may use an actual cereal box that they can apply paper to. If needed, your student may use a mailing cardboard box as an alternative. Have your student cover up the box with different images that pertain to their chosen Civil War figure (i.e., important battles) by using an online search engine or by drawing.

On the sides of the box where one normally finds the nutritional information, ask your student to craft a timeline of key events in this historical figure's life. Encourage creativity by asking your student to create a game, such as a crossword puzzle or word search that relates to the Civil War, on the back of the box. Finally, ask your student to create a name for the cereal.

Answer Key

Write *(Why did the Southern states fear Lincoln's election?)*

Answers will vary. Possible answer: Southern states were afraid that if the western territories eventually became free states, slavery would be outlawed entirely.

Write *(Which strength did the North use to effectively cut the South off from trade and resupply?)*

Answers will vary. Possible answer: The Navy, which was used to blockade Southern ports and control the river trade on the Mississippi, Ohio, Arkansas, and Tennessee rivers.

Write *(What advantage did the Northern forces get from winning Vicksburg from the South?)*

Answers will vary. Possible answer: They won control of the Mississippi River, which cut the Confederacy in half with Texas, Arkansas, and Louisiana cut off from the rest of the states.

Practice *(Graphic Organizer)*

Check your student's sentences or drawings to make sure they are precise and accurate.

Practice *(Major Events of the Civil War)*

Check your student's list of sentences for each major event that highlights its importance or significance. Ensure historical accuracy.

Practice *(The Union vs. the Confederacy)*

Answers will vary. Possible answer:

Union: the president was Abraham Lincoln; included states such as New York, Delaware, Iowa, Illinois, Pennsylvania, and California; was anti-slavery; relied on manufacturing for their economy

Confederacy: the president was Jefferson Davis; states included Louisiana, South Carolina, Texas, Georgia, Alabama, and Mississippi; was pro-slavery; had an economy based on agriculture (enslaved African Americans to work in their cotton fields)

Both: had patriotic soldiers, garnered public support for the Civil War

Quick Review

Refer to the statement your student circled in the Show What You Know section to self-assess their knowledge of the chapter concepts. Then to assist in determining if your student is ready to take the assessment, consider:

- Having your student review the graphic organizer of different vocabulary words in the Practice section.
- Having your student describe the sentence they wrote for each major Civil War event that highlights its importance or significance in the table.
- Having your student describe the differences between the Union and Confederacy and identify some of the similarities between them in the Venn diagram.

Chapter Assessment

Use the words in the Word Bank to complete the sentences.

Word Bank:
abolish   gatling   pardon   Proclamation
secede   ironclad   uprising   Yankee

1. A(n) _____ is the nickname for a person born or living in the northern United States.

2. A(n) _____ was a ship with a metal hull.

3. Some states, such as Louisiana, Alabama, and South Carolina supported slavery and decided to illegally _____ from the United States.

4. After the Civil War, President Lincoln proposed that any southerner who took an oath to the Union would be given a _____.

5. During the Reconstruction era, Union troops occupied much of the South to ensure that laws were followed and that another _____ did not occur.

6. President Lincoln freed slaves in the Southern states in the Emancipation _____.

7. The South was afraid Lincoln would _____ slavery.

8. The _____ gun could fire hundreds of bullets per minute.

Circle the correct answer.

9. This Virginia-born general designed the North's Anaconda Plan.

A. Robert E. Lee   **C.** Winfield Scott

B. Stonewall Jackson   **D.** George Thomas

10. This Virginia-born general was offered command of the Northern Army but ended up fighting for the South.

A. Robert E. Lee   **C.** Winfield Scott

B. Stonewall Jackson   **D.** George Thomas

11. Southern advantages in the war included _____.

A. greater population   **C.** control of the Navy

B. more industrial production   **D.** more experienced generals

12. Northern advantages in the war included _____.

   A. greater food production

   B. more experienced generals

   C. stronger morale

   D. more industrial production

13. The original seven states to secede included _____.

   A. South Carolina

   B. South Dakota

   C. West Virginia

   D. West Texas

14. The following were all border states except _____.

   A. Missouri

   B. Oklahoma

   C. West Virginia

   D. Kentucky

15. Fort Sumter was located in _____.

   A. Louisiana

   B. New Jersey

   C. South Carolina

   D. Georgia

16. The major in charge of Fort Sumter was named _____.

   A. Anderson

   B. Pickens

   C. Buchannan

   D. Lee

17. The first President of the Confederate States of America was _____.

   A. Alexander Stephens

   B. Jefferson Davis

   C. David Jefferson

   D. Robert E. Lee

18. All slaves were freed by the _____.

   A. Emancipation Proclamation

   B. Thirteenth Amendment

   C. Fourteenth Amendment

   D. Fifteenth Amendment

19. Former slaves were clearly granted citizenship and rights by the _____.

   A. Emancipation Proclamation

   B. Thirteenth Amendment

   C. Fourteenth Amendment

   D. Fifteenth Amendment

20. Voting rights of all male citizens regardless of race are protected by _____.

   A. Emancipation Proclamation

   B. Thirteenth Amendment

   C. Fourteenth Amendment

   D. Fifteenth Amendment

Circle True or False.

21. True or False   Lincoln's Reconstruction plan was followed exactly.

22. True or False   Lee won the Battle of Vicksburg.

23. True or False   Sherman's March to the Sea ended in Atlanta

24. True or False   The Battle of Gettysburg turned the tide of the war.

25. True or False   Vicksburg was the last Southern fort on the Mississippi to fall.

26. True or False   President Johnson followed all of Lincoln's policies.

27. True or False   Ironclad warships gave the North an advantage in the war.

28. True or False   Civil War torpedoes could travel faster than ships.

29. True or False   President Johnson changed Lincoln's reconstruction plan.

30. True or False   The Fifteenth Amendment protects voting rights.

Answer the following question in complete sentences.

31. What was the importance of the battles of Vicksburg and Gettysburg?

214

Discover! SOCIAL STUDIES • GRADE 4 • CHAPTER 11 ASSESSMENT

Chapter Assessment Answer Key

1. Yankee
2. ironclad
3. secede
4. pardon
5. uprising
6. Proclamation
7. abolish
8. gatling
9. C
10. A
11. D
12. D
13. A
14. B
15. C
16. A
17. B
18. B
19. C
20. D
21. False
22. False
23. False
24. True
25. True
26. False
27. False
28. False
29. True

30. True
31. Answers will vary. Possible answer: At the Battle of Vicksburg, the Union states captured and controlled the Mississippi River. At the Battle of Gettysburg, it was a turning point in the Civil War. In addition, this was the deadliest battle and was when Lee's plans to take Washington, D.C., were ended.

Alternative Assessment

Project: Infographic

Project Requirements or Steps:

You will create an infographic to show and describe one of the key battles during the Civil War. An infographic is a chart or diagram used to convey information or data quickly and clearly. Use the following steps to create your infographic.

1. Select one of the key battles during the Civil War. Gather information about the features of the event.

2. Create a title for your infographic related to the topic.

3. Include photos and drawings related to the topic.

4. Include information or data to explain and support the photos and drawings you included.

5. Include at least three notable facts about the key battle that you selected. Be sure to describe how the battle impacted American society.

6. Present the information in a creative way.

Alternative Assessment Rubric

Use the following rubric to grade your student's assessment.

	4	3	2	1	Points
Connection to the Unit	The infographic is clearly connected to the unit.	The infographic is connected to the unit.	The infographic is somewhat connected to the unit.	The infographic is not related to the unit.	
Creativity	The infographic is very creative and aesthetically appealing.	The infographic is creative and aesthetically appealing.	The infographic is somewhat creative and aesthetically appealing.	The infographic is not creative or aesthetically appealing.	
Information	The information or data is very accurate and easy to follow.	The information or data is accurate.	The information or data is somewhat accurate.	The information or data is not accurate.	
Grammar and Mechanics	There are no grammar or punctuation mistakes.	There are one or two grammar or punctuation mistakes.	There are several grammar or punctuation mistakes.	There are a distracting number of grammar or punctuation mistakes.	

Total Points _____/16

Average _____

Discover! SOCIAL STUDIES • GRADE 4 • CHAPTER 11 ASSESSMENT

217